IMPORTANT THINGS TO KNOW BEFORE RETIREMENT

A Practical Guide to Financial Security and Fulfillment in Your Golden Years

Copyright

No part of this book may be reproduced, distributed, or transmitted in any form or by any means, including photocopying, recording, or other electronic or mechanical methods, without the prior written permission of the publisher, except in the case of brief quotations embodied in critical reviews and certain other noncommercial uses permitted by copyright law.

All rights reserved ©2024 Delmer Vyncent

Table of Contents

1. Introduction: Preparing for the Retirement Journey
   - The Importance of Early Planning
   - Understanding Your Retirement Goals
   - Assessing Your Current Financial Situation

2. Chapter 1: Financial Foundations for Retirement
   - Calculating Retirement Needs: How Much is Enough?
   - The Power of Compound Interest and Investment Strategies
   - Understanding Retirement Accounts: 401(k), IRA, and Roth IRA

3. Chapter 2: Diversifying Your Retirement Portfolio
   - The Role of Stocks, Bonds, and Mutual Funds
   - Exploring Real Estate as a Retirement Investment
   - Annuities and Other Income Streams

4. Chapter 3: Maximizing Social Security Benefits
   - Understanding Social Security: Eligibility and Benefits
   - Strategies to Maximize Your Social Security Income
   - Navigating the Application Process

5. Chapter 4: Healthcare Planning in Retirement
   - Understanding Medicare: Parts A, B, C, and D
   - Long-Term Care Insurance: Is It Right for You?
   - Managing Healthcare Costs and Selecting the Right Plan

6. Chapter 5: Estate Planning and Legal Considerations
   - Creating a Will and Trust: What You Need to Know
   - Powers of Attorney and Healthcare Directives
   - Strategies for Minimizing Estate Taxes

7. Chapter 6: Redefining Your Lifestyle for Retirement
   - Downsizing: When and How to Make the Move

- Deciding Where to Live: Urban vs. Rural, Domestic vs. International
- Managing Day-to-Day Finances: Budgeting and Living Within Your Means

8. Chapter 7: Staying Active and Healthy in Retirement
- The Importance of Physical Activity and Nutrition
- Mental Wellness: Staying Sharp and Engaged
- Building and Maintaining a Social Network

9. Chapter 8: Navigating the Emotional Transition to Retirement
- Coping with Identity Changes Post-Career
- Finding Purpose and Passion in Your Golden Years
- Strategies for Maintaining Mental and Emotional Health

10. Chapter 9: Exploring Part-Time Work and Volunteer Opportunities
- The Benefits of Part-Time Employment in Retirement
- Finding Meaningful Volunteer Work
- Turning Hobbies into Income Streams

11. Chapter 10: Traveling in Retirement: Planning and Budgeting
- Budget-Friendly Travel Tips and Destinations
- Long-Term Travel and Living Abroad: Pros and Cons
- Health and Travel Insurance for Retirees

12. Chapter 11: Preparing for the Unexpected
- Emergency Funds: How Much Should You Save?
- Dealing with Market Volatility and Economic Downturns
- Adapting Your Retirement Plan to Life's Changes

13. Chapter 12: The Role of Family in Retirement Planning
- Discussing Your Plans with Family Members
- Navigating Financial Support for Adult Children
- Preparing for the Possibility of Becoming a Caregiver

14. Chapter 13: Leveraging Technology to Enhance Retirement

- Online Tools for Managing Finances and Investments
  - Staying Connected with Family and Friends Digitally
  - Learning New Skills and Hobbies Through Technology

15. Chapter 14: Final Steps to a Secure and Fulfilling Retirement
    - Regularly Reviewing and Adjusting Your Retirement Plan
    - Setting New Goals and Celebrating Milestones
    - Building a Legacy: Giving Back and Making a Difference

16. Conclusion: Embracing the Next Chapter of Life
    - Reflecting on Your Accomplishments and Goals
    - Staying Open to New Experiences and Opportunities
    - Encouraging a Positive Outlook on Retirement

17. Appendices
    - Appendix A: Retirement Planning Checklist
    - Appendix B: Resources for Financial Planning and Retirement
    - Appendix C: Recommended Reading and Online tools

Introduction
Preparing for the Retirement Journey

Retirement is one of the most significant milestones in life, marking the shift from years of work to a phase of rest, exploration, and enjoyment. However, this transition can be smooth and fulfilling only when approached with careful planning and foresight. Preparing for retirement involves more than just financial savings; it's about setting goals, understanding your needs, and positioning yourself to live comfortably during your later years.

In this introduction, we'll break down the essentials for preparing your retirement journey by discussing the importance of early planning, understanding your retirement goals, and assessing your current financial situation.

The Importance of Early Planning

Imagine building a house: you wouldn't begin construction without blueprints or materials in place, would you? Retirement planning is much the same—except your "house" is your financial security and future lifestyle. The earlier you start, the better prepared you'll be to meet whatever challenges life throws your way.

Why Start Early?

The most obvious benefit of early retirement planning is time. The sooner you begin, the more opportunities you have to grow your wealth. Compound interest is one of your greatest allies; it's the snowball effect where your investments generate earnings, which in turn create even more earnings.

Consider this: If you start saving $200 a month at age 25, and assume an average annual return of 6%, by age 65, you'll have over $400,000 saved. If you wait until you're 35 to start the same savings plan, you would have only around $200,000 by age 65. That's the power of time!

Assessment: Take a moment to reflect on when you started or plan to start saving for retirement. Do you feel you're on track? If not, what's preventing you from beginning today?

Mitigating Risk Through Early Action

Another reason to start early is risk management. Life is unpredictable, and markets can be volatile. By starting early, you give yourself room to adapt to unforeseen circumstances—whether it's a recession, an unexpected health issue, or a career change. Early planning allows you to make smaller, less painful financial adjustments as needed.

Understanding Your Retirement Goals

Retirement looks different for everyone. For some, it might mean relaxing by the beach, while for others, it could involve traveling the world or even pursuing a second career. Before diving into financial planning, it's essential to have a clear vision of what you want your retirement to look like.

Visualizing Your Retirement Lifestyle

Ask yourself:
- Where do you want to live? Will you stay in your current home, downsize, or move to a different state or country?
- What will you do with your time? Will you focus on hobbies, travel, volunteer work, or even part-time employment?
- What level of financial comfort do you need? Think about the standard of living you expect and the costs associated with it—housing, healthcare, entertainment, and so on.

Having a clear idea of your desired retirement lifestyle helps you estimate how much money you'll need to make those dreams a reality.

Assessment: Jot down a list of things you'd like to do during retirement. Does your current financial situation align with these dreams? If not, how could you adjust your goals?

Balancing Wants and Needs

It's important to balance your "wants" and "needs" in retirement. For example, while you might dream of retiring in a luxury villa, you also need to account for practical considerations like healthcare costs, taxes, and everyday living expenses. Your financial plan should strike a balance between the lifestyle you desire and what is realistically sustainable.

Tip: Start by making a list of your essential expenses—things like housing, utilities, groceries, and healthcare. Then, list your discretionary expenses—travel, dining out, hobbies, etc. This will help you prioritize and find areas where adjustments may be needed.

Assessing Your Current Financial Situation

Before you can create a plan to reach your retirement goals, it's essential to take stock of where you currently stand. Think of this like getting your financial health checkup—it helps you identify gaps and areas of improvement so you can build a stronger plan.

Taking Inventory of Your Assets

Begin by listing all your assets:
- Savings Accounts
- Retirement Accounts (401(k), IRA, etc.)
- Investments (stocks, bonds, mutual funds)
- Real Estate

- Pensions or Annuities

These assets form the foundation of your retirement fund. While it's tempting to focus only on your retirement-specific accounts, remember that all your investments contribute to your financial future.

Assessment: Grab a pen and paper or open a spreadsheet and list all your current assets. Be as detailed as possible. Are there any areas where you feel your savings could be stronger?

Reviewing Your Debt

Debt can be a significant roadblock to a successful retirement. Whether it's a mortgage, credit card debt, student loans, or medical bills, paying off what you owe (or at least minimizing your debt) will ease financial stress during retirement.

Tip: Prioritize high-interest debt, like credit card balances, as these will eat away at your savings faster than other forms of debt.

Assessment: Look at your current debt situation. Are you making regular progress in reducing it? What adjustments can you make to accelerate your debt repayment?

Estimating Future Income

Another key aspect of your current financial assessment is estimating what income you can expect in retirement. This may include:
- Social Security Benefits
- Pension Payments
- Investment Dividends
- Rental Income
- Part-time Employment

Take a close look at these potential income streams. How reliable are they? Will they be enough to support your desired lifestyle?

Assessment: Use an online calculator or speak with a financial advisor to estimate your Social Security benefits and other sources of retirement income. Does this estimation align with your retirement goals?

Conclusion

Preparing for retirement requires a combination of foresight, clear goal-setting, and an honest assessment of your current finances. Starting early and understanding what you want from retirement will give you the direction needed to build a solid financial plan. Taking stock of your assets and income, while managing debt, sets the groundwork for long-term success.

Now is the time to take action, whether you're in your 20s and just starting out, or approaching retirement age and looking to fine-tune your strategy. By being proactive, you're already on the right path to a secure and fulfilling retirement.

Chapter 1

Financial Foundations for Retirement

Planning for retirement can seem like a massive undertaking, but a well-structured financial foundation ensures that your transition into retirement is as smooth as possible. In this chapter, we'll break down the essential elements of retirement planning, from calculating how much you'll need, to understanding key investment strategies and the various retirement accounts available to you. Our goal is to equip you with the knowledge to confidently shape your financial future.

Calculating Retirement Needs: How Much is Enough?

One of the most frequent questions surrounding retirement is, "How much money do I need?" Unfortunately, there isn't a single answer that fits everyone. The amount you need depends on several factors: your current lifestyle, your future plans, and how long you expect to live in retirement.

Start by asking yourself what kind of lifestyle you envision during your retirement. Do you picture yourself traveling extensively, or do you prefer a simpler, quieter life at home? Estimating your future expenses based on the lifestyle you want is the first step toward figuring out your retirement savings target. For instance, someone who enjoys international travel may need more savings than someone who plans to live a more modest lifestyle.

An essential factor to consider is longevity. Advances in healthcare mean people are living longer, so your retirement savings may need to last several decades. A general rule of thumb suggests that you'll need about 70% to 80% of your current annual income to maintain your standard of living during retirement. However, this estimate can vary depending on personal circumstances.

To fine-tune your estimate, take these key elements into account:

- Current Savings: How much have you already saved for retirement? This gives you a starting point.

- Annual Expenses: Estimate your future costs such as housing, healthcare, travel, and hobbies. Remember to consider inflation, which can erode your savings' purchasing power over time.

- Expected Income: Think about any income you'll have during retirement, such as Social Security, pensions, or part-time work. Deduct these from your projected expenses to figure out how much your savings will need to cover.

By carefully analyzing these elements, you can calculate a more personalized savings target. There are also retirement calculators online that can offer a more detailed estimate based on your situation.

The Power of Compound Interest and Investment Strategies

In retirement planning, compound interest is one of the most powerful tools you have. Compound interest is essentially earning interest on your interest, and the longer your money has to grow, the more significant the effect.

Here's how it works: If you invest $500 a month starting at age 30 with an average annual return of 7%, by the time you're 65, you'll have invested $210,000. But, thanks to compound interest, your total savings will have grown to nearly $900,000. In contrast, if you wait until age 40 to start saving the same amount, your total savings will be much lower due to the lost years of compounding.

The lesson here is simple: start saving as early as possible. Even modest contributions can lead to substantial savings over time. If you're getting a later start, you may need to save more aggressively or tweak your investment strategy to catch up.

Speaking of investment strategies, your approach should align with your risk tolerance and how far you are from retirement. Let's break this down:

- Growth Investments: If you have a long time before retirement, you can take on more risk. Growth-oriented investments like stocks often provide higher returns in the long term but come with increased volatility.

- Balanced Portfolio: As retirement gets closer, it's wise to shift toward a balanced portfolio that includes a mix of stocks and bonds. This reduces risk while still offering some growth potential.

- Income-Producing Investments: Once you're in retirement, the focus shifts toward preserving your capital and generating income. Bonds, dividend-paying stocks, and other fixed-income investments can provide a steady income to cover living expenses.

A key element of any investment strategy is diversification. Spread your investments across different asset classes to reduce the risk of market fluctuations negatively impacting your portfolio.

Refining Your Retirement Estimate

Many people use broad estimates to calculate their retirement savings needs, but a detailed, personalized estimate offers much greater accuracy. Here are some additional factors to consider:

1. Healthcare Costs: As you age, healthcare costs are likely to rise. Medicare helps, but it doesn't cover everything. You'll need to factor in premiums, co-pays, prescription drugs, and possible long-term care costs. Some experts recommend earmarking a specific portion of your retirement savings for healthcare expenses.

2. Inflation: Over time, inflation reduces the purchasing power of your money. Prices for everything from groceries to utilities will likely be higher in 20 or 30 years. Accounting for an average inflation rate of 2-3% per year helps you avoid underestimating your future needs.

3. Lifestyle Changes: Your expenses may decrease in some areas, like commuting or business-related costs, but increase in others, such as travel or supporting family members. Consider whether you plan to relocate, and whether that area has a higher or lower cost of living. Adjust your savings accordingly based on the reality of your future plans.

4. Social Security: While Social Security benefits can be helpful, they often cover only a small fraction of retirement expenses. Deciding when to start collecting benefits is crucial. You can begin at 62, but your monthly payments will be reduced. Waiting until age 70 maximizes your monthly payout. This decision directly affects your overall retirement plan.

Compound Interest: The Details Matter

The power of compound interest grows significantly over time, but there are a few practical strategies to maximize its impact:

1. The "Snowball" Effect: Imagine compound interest like a snowball rolling downhill. As it grows, it picks up more snow and becomes larger. In the same way, your interest earns interest, and your savings grow faster with each passing year.

2. Start Early: The earlier you begin saving, the more time your money has to grow. For instance, two people invest $5,000 per year—one starting at age 25 and the other at age 35. Even though both earn the same return, the first person will have much more saved by retirement due to the additional compounding years.

3. Regular Contributions: Making consistent, automatic contributions to your retirement accounts ensures your savings grow steadily. Even small amounts can snowball over time.

4. Reinvest Dividends: If you invest in dividend-paying stocks or funds, reinvest the dividends to buy more shares. This further compounds your savings and accelerates growth.

Understanding Retirement Accounts: 401(k), IRA, and Roth IRA

Retirement accounts are essential for saving, but not all accounts are created equal. Let's explore the different options and their benefits:

1. 401(k): This employer-sponsored account allows you to contribute pre-tax income, lowering your taxable income for that year. The investments grow tax-deferred, meaning you only pay taxes upon withdrawal in retirement. Employer matching contributions can provide an additional boost, so contribute at least enough to take full advantage of any match. However, there are annual contribution limits, so be mindful of maximizing your contributions.

2. IRA (Individual Retirement Account): Unlike a 401(k), an IRA is not tied to your employer. Contributions may be tax-deductible depending on your income and retirement coverage at work, and investments grow tax-deferred. An IRA offers greater flexibility in choosing investments compared to a 401(k).

3. Roth IRA: The major difference here is that contributions are made with after-tax dollars. This means no immediate tax break, but your money grows tax-free, and withdrawals in retirement are also tax-free. If you expect to be in a higher tax bracket in retirement, a Roth IRA offers significant advantages. Additionally, Roth IRAs don't have required minimum distributions (RMDs), allowing your money to grow tax-free for as long as you wish.

Additional Details on Retirement Accounts

1. Employer Matching in 401(k)s: Employer contributions are essentially free money for your retirement. Make sure to understand your company's vesting schedule to ensure you're eligible for full employer matches.

2. Traditional IRA vs. Roth IRA: When deciding between these two, consider your current tax bracket and your expectations for future taxes. If you expect to be in a higher tax bracket later, a Roth IRA's tax-free withdrawals could be the better choice.

3. Required Minimum Distributions (RMDs): Traditional 401(k)s and IRAs require you to begin withdrawing funds at age 72. Failure to take RMDs can result in significant penalties, so it's essential to plan accordingly. However, Roth IRAs do not have RMDs, providing greater flexibility in managing your withdrawals.

By combining a clear understanding of your retirement needs with the power of compound interest and the right investment strategies, you're setting yourself up for a successful retirement.

Chapter 2

Diversifying Your Retirement Portfolio

When it comes to retirement, having a diversified portfolio is crucial. Diversification spreads your risk across various assets, helping protect your investments from market volatility while still providing growth opportunities. In this chapter, we will explore the key components of a diversified retirement portfolio, focusing on the role of stocks, bonds, mutual funds, real estate investments, and alternative income streams such as annuities.

The Role of Stocks, Bonds, and Mutual Funds

1. Stocks: Growth and Risk

Stocks are one of the most common assets in a retirement portfolio, often associated with growth potential. When you buy a stock, you're purchasing a small share of a company. As that company grows and becomes more profitable, the value of your stock increases, giving you capital appreciation over time. Stocks also may pay dividends, offering a steady stream of income along with the potential for growth.

Why Include Stocks?

- Long-term Growth: Historically, stocks have outperformed other asset classes over the long term, making them a solid option for growing your retirement savings.

- Dividend Income: Many companies distribute dividends to shareholders, providing a source of regular income, which is particularly useful during retirement.

However, with growth comes risk. Stocks are subject to market volatility, and the value of your investments can fluctuate widely based on economic factors, company performance, and global events. This makes stocks suitable for younger investors or those with a longer time horizon, as they have more time to ride out the market's ups and downs.

2. Bonds: Stability and Income

Bonds are considered more conservative investments compared to stocks, providing a lower but more predictable return. When you purchase a bond, you're essentially lending money to a corporation or government in exchange for regular interest payments and the return of your principal at the bond's maturity.

Why Include Bonds?

- Reduced Risk: Bonds are less volatile than stocks, making them a safer option, especially as you approach retirement.

- Steady Income: Bonds pay regular interest, which can provide a reliable income stream during retirement.

That said, bonds aren't without risk. Interest rates and inflation can erode bond returns. When interest rates rise, bond prices fall, and inflation may diminish the purchasing power of fixed income. A balanced portfolio should typically include bonds to offset the risks associated with stocks, but the exact proportion will depend on your risk tolerance and time to retirement.

3. Mutual Funds: Instant Diversification

Mutual funds are investment vehicles that pool money from many investors to buy a diversified portfolio of stocks, bonds, or other securities. This instant diversification can lower risk while still providing growth potential. There are various types of mutual funds, from stock-focused to bond-focused, and even balanced funds that invest in both.

Why Include Mutual Funds?

- Diversification: Mutual funds spread your investment across many assets, reducing the risk that comes with holding individual stocks or bonds.

- Professional Management: Mutual funds are managed by professionals who make investment decisions on your behalf, which is useful for those who don't have the time or expertise to manage a portfolio actively.

Mutual funds do come with fees, often referred to as expense ratios, which can eat into your returns over time. However, for many investors, the benefits of diversification and professional management outweigh the costs.

Exploring Real Estate as a Retirement Investment

Real estate is an often overlooked but powerful tool for diversifying a retirement portfolio. Whether you're investing in physical property or real estate investment trusts (REITs), real estate offers both growth potential and steady income.

1. Direct Real Estate Investment: Building Wealth Through Property

Investing in real estate offers both income and growth potential, but it's essential to consider whether direct property ownership is a good fit for your retirement strategy. While owning rental properties can provide a consistent stream of income, there are responsibilities and risks involved.

- Rental Income: If managed well, rental properties can generate significant monthly income. You can charge market-rate rent, and if your property is in a desirable location, the rent can increase over time, keeping pace with inflation.

- Appreciation Potential: Real estate typically appreciates over the long term, which means that your property can increase in value, offering capital gains when you eventually sell.

- Tax Advantages: Real estate investors benefit from various tax deductions, including depreciation, mortgage interest, and maintenance costs, which can reduce your taxable income.

However, real estate investment isn't without challenges. You'll need to manage tenants, perform maintenance, and ensure your properties remain occupied. Additionally, real estate is not as liquid as other investments, meaning it can take time to sell a property if you need cash quickly.

2. Real Estate Investment Trusts (REITs): A Passive Approach to Real Estate

For those who prefer a hands-off approach, investing in REITs is a convenient way to add real estate to your portfolio without directly managing properties. REITs are publicly traded companies that own and manage real estate, and they offer several advantages for retirement investors.

- Diversification: REITs invest in a variety of property types, including commercial, residential, industrial, and healthcare real estate, giving you exposure to different sectors of the economy.

- Liquidity: Unlike physical real estate, REITs can be easily bought and sold on the stock market, providing more flexibility if you need access to your capital.

- Income Generation: REITs are required to pay out 90% of their taxable income in the form of dividends, which makes them an attractive option for retirees seeking steady income.

Whether you choose direct real estate investment or REITs, real estate can be a valuable addition to a diversified retirement portfolio.

Annuities and Other Income Streams

As you transition into retirement, the goal shifts from growing your wealth to generating a steady, reliable income stream. Annuities and other income sources can provide the stability you need during your retirement years.

1. Annuities: Tailoring Guaranteed Income to Your Needs

Annuities can provide you with guaranteed income for life, which is particularly appealing for retirees who want certainty and stability. When you purchase an annuity, you give a lump sum to an insurance company, and in return, they guarantee periodic payments for a set period or for life.

- Fixed Annuities: These provide a guaranteed payout, offering peace of mind with consistent income regardless of market conditions.

- Variable Annuities: The payout for these annuities is linked to the performance of investments, meaning your income could fluctuate depending on how the underlying assets perform.

- Indexed Annuities: These are tied to a stock market index (like the S&P 500), allowing you to potentially benefit from market gains while still enjoying a guaranteed minimum payout.

Annuities are not for everyone, as they can come with high fees, surrender charges, and limited flexibility. Additionally, inflation can erode the purchasing power of fixed annuity payments, so it's important to weigh the pros and cons carefully before committing to an annuity.

2. Other Income Streams: Diversifying Your Retirement Income

In addition to annuities, there are other ways to generate income in retirement:

- Dividends from Stocks and Mutual Funds: Dividend-paying stocks and mutual funds offer the opportunity to receive regular income, while also benefiting from the growth of the underlying investments. Many companies increase their dividends over time, which helps protect against inflation.

- Rental Income: If you own real estate, rental income can be a valuable source of cash flow. Rental income tends to rise with inflation, making it an excellent hedge against rising living costs in retirement.

- Social Security: For most retirees, Social Security forms a significant part of their retirement income. It's essential to understand how Social Security works, including the benefits of delaying payments to maximize your monthly income.

- Pension Payments: If you're lucky enough to have a pension, it can provide reliable, lifelong income. Make sure to understand how your pension benefits are calculated, and whether your payments will keep pace with inflation.

- Part-Time Work: Many retirees find joy and fulfillment in part-time work, whether it's consulting in their field, freelancing, or pursuing a passion project that also brings in extra income. Working part-time in retirement can not only provide additional income but also keep you engaged and mentally active.

Conclusion

Diversifying your retirement portfolio is key to ensuring financial stability during your golden years. By incorporating a variety of assets—stocks, bonds, mutual funds, real estate, annuities, and other income streams—you can create a robust retirement plan that balances growth potential with income security. Remember, as you approach retirement, it's important to regularly review and adjust your portfolio to match your evolving financial goals and risk tolerance.

Chapter 3

Maximizing Social Security Benefits

Social Security is a fundamental element in retirement planning for many Americans, providing a stable source of income during the later years of life. To make the most of this benefit, it's essential to understand how it works, who qualifies, and the strategies available to maximize your benefits. This chapter explores Social Security eligibility and benefits, strategies to boost your Social Security income, and how to effectively navigate the application process.

Understanding Social Security: Eligibility and Benefits

Eligibility Criteria

To qualify for Social Security benefits, several factors must be considered:

1. Work Credits: Social Security benefits are based on your work history. You earn work credits through payroll taxes. To qualify, you must accumulate at least 40 credits, equivalent to about 10 years of work.

2. Full Retirement Age (FRA): Your full retirement age depends on your birth year. For those born between 1943 and 1954, the FRA is 66. It gradually increases for those born later, reaching 67 for those born in 1960 or later.

3. Early Retirement: You can claim Social Security as early as age 62, but doing so reduces your monthly benefit permanently—up to 30% if you claim before your FRA.

4. Delayed Retirement Credits: If you delay claiming Social Security past your FRA, your benefit increases by about 8% per year until age 70, allowing for a significant boost in your payout.

5. Spousal and Survivor Benefits: Spouses, divorced spouses, and survivors may be eligible for benefits. A spouse can receive up to 50% of the primary earner's benefit at FRA, while a survivor can receive up to 100% of their deceased spouse's benefit.

Calculation of Benefits

Social Security benefits are calculated using your 35 highest-earning years. The Social Security Administration (SSA) adjusts these earnings for inflation and calculates your average indexed monthly earnings (AIME). The AIME is used to determine your primary insurance amount (PIA), which is the benefit you'll receive at your full retirement age.

Strategies to Maximize Your Social Security Income

Maximizing Social Security benefits involves strategic planning. Here are several methods to help increase your monthly income.

1. Delaying Benefits Until Age 70 One of the best ways to maximize Social Security is to delay claiming your benefits until age 70. Your monthly payout increases by about 8% each year after your full retirement age, up to 70. This can provide a substantial increase in your overall benefit.

2. Working Longer to Increase Your Benefit Since Social Security benefits are based on your highest 35 years of earnings, working longer can help replace lower-earning years with higher-earning ones. This will ultimately increase your monthly benefit when you do claim.

3. Coordinating Spousal Benefits If you're married, coordinating benefits with your spouse can significantly impact your household's overall Social Security income. For example, the lower-earning spouse can claim benefits at full retirement age, while the higher-earning spouse delays their claim until age 70, increasing the household's total benefit.

4. Utilizing Survivor Benefits Survivor benefits can provide essential income for widows or widowers. If your spouse passes away, you may be eligible for up to 100% of their Social Security benefit. When planning for retirement, consider how to maximize survivor benefits for the surviving spouse.

5. Claiming Early and Investing the Benefits Some individuals opt to claim Social Security early and invest the payments, hoping to generate additional returns. However, this approach carries risks, as investment returns are not guaranteed, and you face a permanent reduction in your Social Security benefit by claiming early.

6. Tax Considerations Depending on your total income in retirement, a portion of your Social Security benefits may be subject to federal taxes. If your income exceeds certain thresholds, up to 85% of your benefits could be taxable. Careful tax planning can help reduce the impact of taxes on your Social Security income.

Further Strategies to Maximize Your Social Security Income

In addition to delaying benefits and coordinating with a spouse, here are additional strategies to consider.

1. Consider Working While Collecting Benefits You can begin receiving Social Security benefits as early as age 62 while continuing to work. However, if you are younger than your FRA and earn more than $21,240 (for 2024), your benefits will be temporarily reduced by $1 for every $2 you earn above the limit. After reaching full retirement age, there's no limit on earnings, and your benefits will no longer be reduced.

2. Understanding the Impact of Medicare on Social Security When you enroll in Medicare, Part B premiums are often deducted directly from your Social Security benefits, reducing your monthly payout. This is important to consider when planning how your benefits will fit into your overall retirement strategy.

3. Claiming Benefits as a Divorced Spouse If you were married for at least 10 years and are now divorced, you may be eligible to claim Social Security benefits based on your ex-spouse's earnings. This can provide a valuable source of income in retirement, especially if your ex-spouse had higher earnings than you.

Addressing Common Social Security Myths

Many misconceptions about Social Security can lead to poor decision-making. Let's debunk a few common myths:

1. Myth: Social Security Will Cover All Your Retirement Needs Social Security typically replaces about 40% of pre-retirement income, so relying solely on it for retirement is not advisable. You'll need other income sources like savings or pensions.

2. Myth: Social Security Benefits Are Tax-Free Depending on your overall income, up to 85% of your Social Security benefits could be taxable. If your income exceeds $25,000 (single filers) or $32,000 (married couples), a portion of your benefits will be taxed.

3. Myth: You Must Stop Working to Claim Social Security You can continue working while receiving Social Security benefits, but if you're below FRA, your benefits might be reduced if your earnings exceed the annual limit. Once you reach FRA, there are no earning restrictions.

4. Myth: Social Security Will Run Out of Money While Social Security's trust fund may face future challenges, ongoing payroll taxes will still provide a significant portion of benefits. However, reforms may be needed to prevent reductions.

Navigating the Application Process

Once you've determined the optimal time to claim your benefits, you must navigate the application process carefully to avoid delays or mistakes.

1. When to Apply It's advisable to apply for Social Security benefits about three months before you want payments to start. You can apply online, by phone, or in person at a Social Security office.

2. Documents You'll Need To apply, you will need:

- Your Social Security number

- Proof of age

- Work history details (W-2 forms, tax returns)

- Bank account information for direct deposit

- Marriage or death certificates if applying for spousal or survivor benefits

3. Online vs. In-Person Application

Online Application: The SSA offers a user-friendly online application process. By creating an account on the SSA website, you can apply, track the status of your application, and manage your benefits online from the comfort of your home. This method is convenient and allows you to make updates, track changes, and ensure that everything is handled without needing an office visit.

In-Person Application: If you prefer a face-to-face experience or have a more complex situation—such as needing to apply for spousal or survivor benefits or dealing with special documentation needs—visiting a local Social Security office may be a better option. This approach allows for direct interaction with an SSA representative, which can be helpful if you have specific questions or concerns.

Regardless of the method you choose, double-checking the accuracy of your work history and personal details is crucial to avoid mistakes that could delay your application or affect your benefits.

4. Receiving Your Benefits Once your application is approved, payments will be made monthly, either through direct deposit or a pre-paid debit card. Benefits are paid in arrears, meaning you'll receive your payment for the previous month.

5. Handling Delays or Discrepancies If there are any issues with your payments or application, it's important to contact the SSA immediately. Regularly reviewing your Social Security statement can help catch errors in your earnings history that might impact your benefits.

6. Appealing a Decision If your application is denied, you can appeal the decision. There are four levels of appeal, starting with reconsideration and going all the way to federal court review, if necessary.

Conclusion

Maximizing your Social Security benefits requires careful planning and an understanding of how the system works. By considering when to claim, coordinating spousal benefits, understanding the tax implications, and ensuring accurate application, you can optimize your Social Security income. With thoughtful strategies and a comprehensive approach, Social Security can provide a solid foundation for your retirement years.

Chapter 4

Healthcare Planning in Retirement

When thinking about retirement, many of us envision relaxation, travel, and leisure. However, one crucial area that often gets overlooked is healthcare planning. Ensuring your health needs are adequately met can prevent a strain on your financial resources and offer peace of mind. This chapter will dive into understanding Medicare, evaluating long-term care insurance, and strategies for managing healthcare costs in retirement.

Understanding Medicare: Parts A, B, C, and D

Medicare, the federal health insurance program for those 65 and older, has four key parts that can be confusing at first glance. But understanding how each part works is crucial for making informed decisions about your retirement healthcare plan.

Medicare Part A (Hospital Insurance):

Part A is often referred to as hospital insurance, covering inpatient care in hospitals, skilled nursing facilities, hospice, and some home healthcare. If you've worked and paid Medicare taxes for at least 10 years, you won't need to pay premiums for Part A. However, you may still face out-of-pocket costs like deductibles or co-pays.

Imagine being hospitalized for an unexpected illness or injury. Part A will help cover the cost of your stay and post-hospital rehabilitation, but keep in mind that longer stays or more complex treatments can lead to additional expenses that are not covered.

Medicare Part B (Medical Insurance):

Part B covers outpatient care, doctor visits, preventive services, and medical equipment. Unlike Part A, there's a monthly premium for Part B, determined by your income level. There are also deductibles and co-insurance payments, which are out-of-pocket costs for services like doctor's visits or lab tests.

Consider a scenario where you need regular check-ups or specialized care. Medicare Part B helps cover the costs of these visits and treatments, but the premium, co-pays, and other costs can add up over time. Budgeting for these expenses is critical.

Medicare Part C (Medicare Advantage Plans):

Medicare Advantage, or Part C, is a private insurance option that includes Parts A and B, and usually prescription drug coverage. These plans often provide additional benefits such as vision, dental, and hearing coverage. However, they may limit you to a network of healthcare providers.

Think of Part C as a one-stop-shop for your Medicare needs. It offers more comprehensive coverage, but the trade-off is that you may need to stay within a network of providers. It's essential to weigh the convenience of all-in-one coverage with the potential restrictions.

Medicare Part D (Prescription Drug Coverage):

Part D is a stand-alone plan that helps cover the cost of prescription medications. Similar to Part B, it comes with a monthly premium, and the costs vary based on the plan you select and the medications you require.

Consider a chronic condition where you rely on daily medications. Without Part D, the cost of these medications can quickly become unmanageable. Reviewing your prescriptions annually ensures your plan remains cost-effective and provides the coverage you need.

Additional Considerations for Medicare

Enrollment Deadlines and Penalties:

It's critical to enroll in Medicare on time to avoid penalties that can follow you throughout retirement. If you miss your initial enrollment period at age 65, particularly for Part B, you could face a lifelong penalty that increases your premiums by 10% for each year you were eligible but didn't sign up.

Imagine relying on employer-sponsored insurance past age 65 and missing the transition to Medicare. This mistake could cost you significantly in higher premiums. Planning your enrollment carefully will help avoid these financial burdens.

Medigap (Medicare Supplement Insurance):

For retirees who choose Original Medicare (Parts A and B), a Medigap policy can be helpful. Medigap is sold by private insurers and covers out-of-pocket costs like co-pays, deductibles, and co-insurance. However, Medigap does not cover long-term care, dental, or vision services.

The best time to purchase a Medigap policy is during your open enrollment period, which begins when you turn 65 and are enrolled in Part B. During this time, you can purchase any Medigap policy available in your state, regardless of pre-existing conditions. After this period, it becomes harder and more expensive to get a Medigap policy if you have health issues.

Long-Term Care Insurance: Is It Right for You?

Long-term care is one of the most pressing concerns for retirees. As we age, we may need help with daily tasks such as bathing, dressing, or eating, which can be provided either at home or in a long-term care facility. However, these services are not covered by Medicare, leaving retirees vulnerable to high costs unless they plan for long-term care.

Cost of Long-Term Care:

On average, the cost of a private room in a nursing home exceeds $100,000 per year. In-home care, depending on the services needed, can range from $4,000 to $10,000 per month. This can quickly deplete your savings if not properly planned for.

Long-term care insurance helps cover these costs, but premiums can be expensive. The younger and healthier you are when you purchase it (typically in your mid-50s or early 60s), the lower your premiums will be.

Hybrid Policies: A Flexible Option

Hybrid long-term care policies, which combine life insurance with long-term care coverage, have become increasingly popular. If you don't use the long-term care benefit, your beneficiaries will receive a death benefit. These policies can be a more flexible option than traditional long-term care insurance, which is often a "use it or lose it" policy.

This hybrid approach gives peace of mind: if you don't need long-term care, your investment in the policy is still passed on to your family.

When Should You Buy Long-Term Care Insurance?

The best time to buy long-term care insurance is in your mid-50s to early 60s, when you're still healthy and premiums are manageable. Waiting too long can result in higher premiums or denial of coverage due to pre-existing conditions.

Just as you wouldn't wait to buy homeowner's insurance until your house catches fire, don't delay purchasing long-term care insurance until you need care. Planning ahead ensures that you have a financial safeguard in place when you need it most.

Managing Healthcare Costs and Selecting the Right Plan

Healthcare costs in retirement can be unpredictable, but taking a proactive approach can help mitigate potential financial strain.

Step 1: Assess Your Healthcare Needs

Begin by evaluating your health and family history. Are there any chronic conditions that require ongoing care? Do you anticipate needing frequent doctor visits or surgeries in the future? Understanding these factors will guide you in selecting the right plan.

For example, if heart disease runs in your family, look for a plan that offers robust cardiovascular care coverage. If you regularly take prescription medications, prioritize a plan that offers lower out-of-pocket costs for drugs.

Step 2: Research Available Plans

Whether you're considering Original Medicare or Medicare Advantage, compare the benefits, costs, and provider networks. Original Medicare offers more freedom in choosing providers, but Medicare Advantage plans often bundle services, like prescription drugs and vision care, in one convenient package.

Take time to explore the options in your area. Consult a licensed Medicare specialist to help you compare plans and understand which one is most appropriate for your healthcare needs.

Step 3: Factor in Prescription Drug Coverage

Prescription drug costs can be a significant expense. Medicare Part D or Medicare Advantage plans with drug coverage can help reduce these costs. Check the formulary (the list of covered drugs) annually to ensure your medications are still covered, and explore options like generic alternatives to save on costs.

Some plans have "donut holes" or coverage gaps where you're required to pay more for medications. Be sure to understand how these coverage gaps could affect your budget.

Step 4: Prepare for the Unexpected

Medical emergencies can arise without warning, and they often come with high costs. Consider setting up a health savings account (HSA) before retirement or maintaining a liquid emergency fund to cover healthcare expenses Medicare doesn't pay for.

Additionally, a Medigap policy can help cover unexpected out-of-pocket costs that aren't covered by Original Medicare, such as deductibles and co-insurance. Though it adds a monthly premium, it can protect you from significant financial strain in the event of a health crisis.

The Importance of Staying Informed

Healthcare plans and policies change from year to year. It's essential to stay informed about Medicare updates and evaluate your plan annually. As your health evolves, so too should your healthcare plan. Regular reviews during the Medicare open enrollment period ensure that you're always receiving the best care at the most reasonable cost.

Final Thoughts

Healthcare planning in retirement requires thoughtful preparation. Understanding Medicare, considering long-term care insurance, and managing healthcare costs are vital to safeguarding your health and finances. With these tools in hand, you'll be well-equipped to navigate the healthcare challenges of retirement and enjoy your golden years with confidence and peace of mind.

Chapter 5

Estate Planning and Legal Considerations

When planning for retirement, ensuring that your healthcare and financial needs are covered is essential, but it's also important to think about how you want your assets managed and distributed after you're gone. Estate planning allows you to ensure that your legacy is preserved, your loved ones are taken care of, and your wishes are respected. In this chapter, we'll cover the essential elements of estate planning, including creating a will and trust, the role of powers of attorney and healthcare directives, and strategies to minimize estate taxes.

Creating a Will and Trust: What You Need to Know

Let's start with the basics: a will and a trust. These are the foundational documents in any estate plan, but they serve different purposes, and knowing how they work will help you decide which is right for you—or if you need both.

The Will: Ensuring Your Wishes Are Followed

A will is a legal document that details how you want your assets—such as money, property, and personal belongings—distributed after your death. Without a will, your estate will be distributed according to your state's laws, which may not align with your wishes. A will also allows you to name an executor, the person responsible for carrying out your instructions, and, if you have minor children, it can designate a guardian.

Imagine not having a will. It leaves your loved ones with uncertainty during an already emotional time. For instance, without clear instructions, disputes could arise over who gets what, and the court may end up deciding for you. A well-drafted will ensures that your wishes are honored and reduces stress on your family.

The Trust: Avoiding Probate and Protecting Privacy

A trust is a more flexible estate planning tool that can be used to manage your assets during your lifetime and distribute them after your death. One of the biggest advantages of a trust is that it allows your estate to bypass probate—a public legal process where a will is validated, and the estate is settled. Probate can be time-consuming, expensive, and exposes your private affairs to the public.

With a trust, you can also specify how and when your assets should be distributed. For instance, if you want your children to receive their inheritance only after they reach a certain age or milestone, a trust allows you to set those conditions.

Trusts come in different forms:

- Revocable Trusts can be changed or revoked during your lifetime.

- Irrevocable Trusts cannot be altered once created, but they offer stronger asset protection and tax benefits.

Trusts provide greater control, flexibility, and privacy, making them ideal if you have a complex estate or specific distribution instructions. By setting up a trust, you're making it easier for your heirs to inherit what you've worked hard to accumulate without delays or legal hurdles.

Which One Should You Choose?

Most people benefit from having both a will and a trust. While a will is simpler to create, a trust offers added benefits of avoiding probate and protecting privacy. A will is still necessary to cover any assets that aren't included in the trust and to handle personal matters, like appointing guardianship for minor children.

Powers of Attorney and Healthcare Directives

What happens if you're unable to make decisions for yourself due to illness or incapacity? This is where powers of attorney and healthcare directives come in.

Powers of Attorney: Who Will Make Decisions for You?

A power of attorney (POA) is a legal document that gives someone else (your agent or attorney-in-fact) the authority to act on your behalf in financial or legal matters. There are different types of POAs, and it's important to choose the right one based on your needs:

- Durable Power of Attorney: This allows your agent to manage your finances, property, and other affairs if you become incapacitated. Unlike a regular POA, which becomes void if you become mentally incompetent, a durable POA remains in effect.

- Limited Power of Attorney: This grants your agent authority for specific tasks, such as selling property or managing a particular financial transaction, and is often used for a limited time.

By assigning someone as your POA, you are ensuring that your affairs are handled by a trusted individual when you're unable to manage them yourself. Without one, a court may have to appoint a guardian or conservator, which can be a lengthy and expensive process.

Healthcare Directives: Ensuring Your Medical Wishes Are Honored

A healthcare directive (or living will) is a legal document that outlines your medical care preferences if you are unable to communicate them yourself. This could include instructions regarding life-sustaining treatment, resuscitation, or organ donation.

For example, if you were to fall into a coma and had a healthcare directive in place, your family would not be left guessing about your preferences regarding life support. You can also appoint a healthcare proxy, a person you trust to make medical decisions on your behalf based on your stated preferences.

It's uncomfortable to think about, but having these documents ensures that your medical and financial wishes are respected. It also spares your family from making tough decisions without guidance, which can lead to disagreements or guilt.

Strategies for Minimizing Estate Taxes

Estate taxes can significantly reduce the inheritance you leave to your loved ones, but with proper planning, you can reduce the tax burden on your estate.

The Federal Estate Tax Threshold

The good news is that most estates won't be subject to federal estate taxes. As of 2024, estates valued under $13.06 million for individuals ($26.12 million for couples) are exempt from federal estate taxes. However, if your estate exceeds this amount, the excess could be taxed at rates as high as 40%.

Let's say you have a sizable estate that exceeds the federal threshold. Without careful planning, your heirs could lose a significant portion of their inheritance to taxes. This is where strategic estate planning comes in.

Gifting as a Tax Strategy

One of the simplest ways to reduce estate taxes is through gifting. The IRS allows you to gift up to $17,000 per year (as of 2024) to as many individuals as you like, without incurring any gift taxes. This means you can transfer wealth to your loved ones gradually, reducing the overall size of your taxable estate.

Consider this: If you have three children and you gift each of them $17,000 annually, you're reducing your estate by $51,000 every year, potentially saving your heirs from significant estate tax liability down the road.

Charitable Donations

If you're charitably inclined, making donations to nonprofit organizations can also help reduce your taxable estate. Not only do you support causes that matter to you, but these donations can be deducted from your estate, lowering its value and potentially reducing the estate tax burden.

For example, if you donate a portion of your estate to a charity, that value is subtracted from the estate's total before taxes are applied. This can be a meaningful way to leave a legacy while also providing tax benefits.

Trusts for Reducing Taxes

Certain types of trusts, such as irrevocable life insurance trusts (ILITs) and grantor retained annuity trusts (GRATs), can also help minimize estate taxes. By transferring assets to these trusts, you effectively remove them from your taxable estate, while still providing for your beneficiaries.

For instance, an ILIT allows you to transfer life insurance policies into a trust, so when you pass away, the proceeds of the policy are excluded from your taxable estate. This strategy can be especially useful for individuals with large life insurance policies that would otherwise increase the estate's value.

Practical Applications of Estate Planning Tools

Understanding the tools of estate planning—wills, trusts, powers of attorney, healthcare directives, and tax strategies—is only the beginning. The real value comes in knowing how to apply them in ways that meet your specific needs and the needs of your loved ones. Let's explore practical examples of how these tools can work together to protect your assets, manage your care, and ensure your wishes are honored.

Using a Will and Trust Together

Scenario 1: Protecting Your Minor Children

Let's imagine you're a parent with young children. Naturally, you want to ensure that they're taken care of if something happens to you. Here's how a will and trust could work together in your estate plan.

In your will, you appoint a guardian who will care for your children until they reach adulthood. This is essential because, without a guardian named, the court will make that decision, which might not align with your wishes. Your will would also designate how your assets should be distributed to support your children.

However, children are typically not legally able to manage significant assets until they reach a certain age. This is where a trust becomes invaluable. Instead of giving your children their inheritance all at once, you can use a trust to stagger the distribution over time. For example, the trust might give them access to a portion of the funds when they turn 18, another portion when they turn 25, and the rest when they reach 30. You can also give your appointed trustee the discretion to distribute funds earlier for essential expenses, like education or medical needs.

This arrangement ensures that your children are provided for but also protects them from spending their entire inheritance too early.

Scenario 2: Managing Wealth After Your Death

Let's consider a second example, where you're a high-net-worth individual with significant investments and real estate. You want to ensure that your wealth is distributed efficiently, without delays or unnecessary legal challenges.

In this case, a revocable living trust is an excellent tool. During your lifetime, you can manage your assets within the trust and make adjustments as needed. Upon your death, the assets in the trust can be transferred directly to your beneficiaries without going through probate—a process that can be lengthy and costly.

For example, if you own multiple properties, these can be placed in the trust. Upon your death, your trustee would have the authority to manage or sell the properties, distributing the proceeds to your beneficiaries according to your instructions. Since the trust avoids probate, the process is quicker and more private, ensuring that your family's financial affairs aren't exposed in court proceedings.

Practical Use of Powers of Attorney and Healthcare Directives

Scenario 3: Planning for Incapacity

Imagine you're in your late 60s and, while still healthy, you're concerned about the possibility of developing dementia in the future. You want to make sure that if you become incapacitated, someone you trust will handle your financial and medical decisions. This is where powers of attorney and healthcare directives play a crucial role.

First, you create a durable power of attorney for finances. This document names your adult daughter as the person who will handle your financial affairs if you become unable to manage them yourself. For example, she would have the authority to pay your bills, manage your investments, and even sell property on your behalf if necessary.

At the same time, you draft a healthcare directive (or living will) and designate a healthcare proxy. Let's say your preference is to avoid life-prolonging treatments if you're in a permanent vegetative state. The healthcare directive outlines your wishes, and your healthcare proxy, your spouse, would have the authority to make medical decisions in line with those instructions.

By taking these steps, you remove uncertainty and give your loved ones clear guidance on how to act on your behalf if you're ever unable to communicate your wishes. This not only ensures that your preferences are respected, but also helps your family avoid potentially painful or divisive decisions.

Minimizing Estate Taxes with Practical Strategies

Scenario 4: Gifting to Reduce Taxable Estate

Let's say you're in your early 70s, and you've built a successful business that has significantly increased your wealth. You want to reduce the size of your estate to minimize future estate taxes, while also benefiting your children and grandchildren during your lifetime.

One effective strategy is to start an annual gifting program. As mentioned earlier, the IRS allows you to gift up to $17,000 per year (as of 2024) to as many individuals as you like, without incurring any gift tax.

Imagine you have two children and four grandchildren. By gifting each of them $17,000 per year, you can transfer a total of $102,000 out of your estate each year ($17,000 x 6 individuals). Over a decade, that's more than a million dollars transferred to your loved ones without reducing their future inheritance or triggering gift taxes.

This not only reduces the taxable value of your estate, but it also allows your children and grandchildren to enjoy financial support while you're still alive. You can even combine these gifts with other tax-advantaged strategies, such as contributing to 529 education savings plans for your grandchildren.

Scenario 5: Using Charitable Giving for Estate Planning

Another tax-efficient strategy is charitable giving. Let's imagine that you're passionate about supporting education and healthcare. You can use charitable donations to not only support causes you care about but also reduce the size of your taxable estate.

For example, you could set up a charitable remainder trust (CRT). In this arrangement, you transfer assets—such as appreciated stocks or real estate—into the trust. The CRT provides you or your beneficiaries with income for a set period, after which the remaining assets are donated to your chosen charity. This allows you to support a cause you care about while receiving a charitable deduction and reducing the size of your taxable estate.

Additionally, by donating appreciated assets, you avoid paying capital gains taxes on those assets, which can be a significant benefit if they have grown substantially in value over time.

Scenario 6: Using an Irrevocable Life Insurance Trust (ILIT)

Life insurance can also create estate tax burdens if the policy is part of your taxable estate. To avoid this, high-net-worth individuals often establish an Irrevocable Life Insurance Trust (ILIT). By transferring ownership of your life insurance policy to the ILIT, the policy's death benefit is removed from your taxable estate.

Here's how it works: You set up an ILIT, transfer your existing life insurance policy into the trust, and designate beneficiaries—such as your spouse or children—who will receive the proceeds upon your death. Since the policy is no longer part of your estate, the death benefit is not subject to estate taxes. This strategy is particularly useful if you have a large life insurance policy that could push the value of your estate above the federal estate tax threshold.

Multi-Generational Estate Planning

Scenario 7: Creating a Legacy with a Dynasty Trust

Let's say you're a grandparent with substantial wealth, and you want to ensure that your grandchildren and great-grandchildren are provided for, while also protecting the family wealth from creditors or lawsuits. In this case, you might consider setting up a dynasty trust.

A dynasty trust is designed to last for multiple generations. It allows you to transfer assets—such as real estate or investments—to the trust, which can provide income and support for your descendants for decades to come. Since the assets in the trust are not part of the beneficiaries' personal estates, they're protected from creditors and, in some cases, estate taxes for several generations.

For instance, you might establish a dynasty trust that provides funds for your grandchildren's college education, while also preserving the bulk of the trust assets for future generations. By using a dynasty trust, you can leave a lasting legacy that benefits your family long after you're gone.

Conclusion

Estate planning is not just about protecting your wealth—it's about preserving your legacy, taking care of your loved ones, and ensuring that your wishes are carried out. Whether you're creating a simple will, setting up a trust, or implementing tax-saving strategies, the right combination of tools can make a world of difference.

Through practical examples like setting up trusts for minor children, establishing powers of attorney, gifting to minimize taxes, or using charitable trusts to create lasting impact, you can see how these strategies work together to meet your estate planning goals.

By starting the process now, you can ensure that your estate is managed according to your wishes, with minimal tax burdens and legal complications, allowing you to leave a meaningful legacy for your family and the causes you care about.

Chapter 6

Redefining Your Lifestyle for Retirement

As you transition into retirement, a new chapter of life unfolds, bringing both excitement and a need for careful planning. Retirement is not just about leaving your career behind; it's about rediscovering and reshaping your lifestyle to align with your new reality. In this chapter, we'll explore the essential elements that can help you redefine your lifestyle for a fulfilling retirement. Whether it's downsizing your home, deciding where to live, or managing your daily finances, the decisions you make now will set the stage for years to come.

Downsizing: When and How to Make the Move

Downsizing can be an emotional and practical decision. As children move out and you find yourself with more space than you need, the idea of downsizing may become appealing. The goal of downsizing is to simplify your living environment, reduce maintenance responsibilities, and cut expenses.

When to Downsize

Deciding when to downsize depends on personal circumstances and readiness. Some may choose to downsize right as they retire, while others may delay the decision until later. Signs that it might be time to consider downsizing include:

- High maintenance costs and effort for your current home

- Empty rooms or spaces that no longer serve a purpose

- Desire to free up capital for travel, healthcare, or other needs

- Physical challenges in navigating a larger home (such as stairs or yard work)

It's important to remember that downsizing doesn't have to be rushed. Give yourself time to plan the move, emotionally process leaving a home filled with memories, and research what kind of living arrangement will best fit your new lifestyle.

How to Downsize

The downsizing process can feel overwhelming, but approaching it in manageable steps helps alleviate stress:

1. Start Early: Begin sorting through belongings well in advance of the move. Consider what you want to keep, sell, donate, or throw away.

2. Declutter: Evaluate your possessions based on whether they add value to your life. Sentimental items may be tough to part with, but ask yourself if they still serve a meaningful purpose.

3. Assess Your New Space: Look at the floor plan of your new home and determine how much furniture you'll need. A smaller home means less storage, so plan accordingly.

4. Hire Help if Needed: Consider hiring a moving service or a professional downsizing consultant who can help you stay organized and focused.

5. Stay Positive: Downsizing is an opportunity to make your home more manageable and your life simpler, freeing up energy and resources for more fulfilling experiences.

Deciding Where to Live: Urban vs. Rural, Domestic vs. International

Where you live in retirement can greatly influence your quality of life, daily activities, and financial security. This decision can be shaped by several factors, including health needs, proximity to family, cost of living, and lifestyle preferences. Let's explore some key considerations when deciding where to live.

Urban vs. Rural

- Urban Living: Cities offer convenience, access to healthcare, cultural events, and public transportation. Urban living is ideal for those who enjoy being close to amenities like restaurants, theaters, and museums. However, the cost of living in cities can be high, and the hustle and bustle may feel overwhelming for those seeking peace and quiet.

- Rural Living: Moving to a rural area provides a slower pace of life, wide open spaces, and a close-knit community. The cost of living is generally lower, making it an attractive option for retirees looking to stretch their budget. On the downside, rural areas may have limited access to medical facilities and entertainment options, and you may need a car to get around.

Domestic vs. International

- Domestic: Staying in your home country during retirement offers familiarity and ease of access to family and friends. You understand the healthcare system, tax laws, and social services. If you plan to move to a new area domestically, you can still choose a different climate or lifestyle (for example, moving from a cold region to a warmer one).

- International: Some retirees seek adventure and lower living costs by moving abroad. Countries in Central America, Southeast Asia, and Europe have become popular retirement destinations due to affordable healthcare and housing. However, international relocation comes with challenges like navigating a new healthcare system, potential language barriers, and being far from family. It's essential to carefully research the legal and financial implications of retiring overseas, including visa requirements, cost of living, and quality of healthcare.

Whether you choose urban, rural, domestic, or international living, make sure the decision reflects your personal values, hobbies, and comfort level. It's also important to visit potential destinations, spend time there, and gather feedback from current residents.

Managing Day-to-Day Finances: Budgeting and Living Within Your Means

Financial management is crucial during retirement. Unlike in your working years, where you could rely on a steady paycheck, you'll now be living on a fixed income, which requires careful budgeting to ensure long-term financial stability.

Creating a Retirement Budget

A well-crafted budget allows you to plan for both day-to-day expenses and unforeseen costs. Start by reviewing your monthly income from sources like Social Security, pensions, and investment withdrawals. Then, list your essential expenses (housing, food, healthcare, insurance) and discretionary spending (entertainment, travel).

1. Track Your Spending: Use budgeting tools or apps to monitor where your money goes. By understanding your spending habits, you can adjust and allocate funds more effectively.

2. Plan for Healthcare Costs: Medical expenses tend to rise with age, so include Medicare premiums, supplemental insurance, and out-of-pocket expenses in your budget.

3. Prioritize Savings: Even in retirement, setting aside a portion of your income for unexpected emergencies is important.

4. Reevaluate Your Budget Regularly: Your financial needs may change over time. Keep your budget flexible, and review it annually to ensure it meets your evolving lifestyle.

Living Within Your Means

Living within your means is essential to avoid dipping into your savings too early. Some strategies to help include:

- Downsizing Your Lifestyle: If your budget is tight, consider cutting non-essential expenses, such as subscription services or dining out frequently.

- Frugal Living: Look for discounts and deals, whether it's senior discounts at restaurants, travel packages, or memberships at local clubs.

- Debt Management: Entering retirement with debt can weigh heavily on your financial security. Focus on paying down high-interest debt and avoid accumulating new loans.

- Supplemental Income: Some retirees opt for part-time work, consulting, or starting a small business to supplement their retirement income. This can help you avoid depleting your savings too quickly and provide a sense of purpose.

By staying mindful of your finances and living within your means, you can enjoy a more comfortable and stress-free retirement, free from the worries of outliving your money.

Conclusion

Redefining your lifestyle in retirement involves thoughtful choices about downsizing, selecting the right living environment, and managing your day-to-day finances. Each decision should be made with an eye toward long-term fulfillment, financial security, and personal well-being. By taking the time to carefully plan and adapt, you can enjoy a lifestyle that allows you to savor your retirement years with peace of mind and confidence.

Chapter 7

Staying Active and Healthy in Retirement

Retirement is often seen as the "golden years"—a time to relax and enjoy the fruits of decades of hard work. However, staying active and healthy during this period is essential for making the most of these years. It's easy to fall into the trap of a sedentary lifestyle once you no longer have the routine of work. But just because you're not working doesn't mean you should stop moving or challenging yourself mentally and socially. In this chapter, we'll dive into the importance of physical activity and nutrition, how to maintain mental sharpness, and the vital role social connections play in a healthy retirement.

The Importance of Physical Activity and Nutrition

Physical activity is like the foundation of a house: it supports everything else in your life. In retirement, staying physically active doesn't just help you look and feel good—it can enhance your mobility, prevent chronic illnesses, and improve your mood. Whether you're running, walking, gardening, or doing yoga, movement keeps your body functioning at its best.

Why You Need Physical Activity More Than Ever

Physical activity helps with flexibility, muscle strength, balance, and endurance. As we age, maintaining these areas becomes even more critical to prevent falls, maintain independence, and keep energy levels high. Think about Alice, a 70-year-old retiree who enjoys her morning yoga routine. She attributes her ability to keep up with her grandkids and enjoy long walks with friends to staying consistent with her yoga. In her words, "If I don't move it, I lose it!"

The key isn't in intense workouts, but rather in staying consistent with any kind of movement that gets your body going. Daily walks, low-impact exercises, or even gardening can have profound effects on your overall health.

Practical Physical Activity Ideas

- Walking: Walking is one of the best forms of exercise. It's low-impact and can be easily integrated into your daily routine. Try setting a goal for a 30-minute walk every day.

- Stretching and Flexibility: Practices like yoga or simple stretching routines help maintain mobility and flexibility. These activities can be done at home, requiring only a small mat or towel.

- Strength Training: Lifting light weights or using resistance bands helps maintain muscle mass, which is crucial for bone health. This can be as simple as using household items like water bottles or canned food.

- Group Activities: Group fitness classes for seniors are a great way to stay active and socialize. Swimming, water aerobics, or Zumba classes designed for older adults are popular options.

The Role of Nutrition in Staying Active

Along with physical activity, proper nutrition is the other side of the coin. As you age, your body needs fewer calories, but more nutrients to stay healthy. Eating a well-balanced diet helps fuel your activity levels and supports your body in repairing tissues, building strength, and fighting off diseases.

Take Bob, for instance. After retiring, he noticed that his energy levels were dipping, and he was gaining weight despite being moderately active. After consulting a nutritionist, he swapped out processed snacks for fruits, whole grains, and lean proteins. Within weeks, Bob felt lighter, more energetic, and was sleeping better.

Practical Nutrition Tips for Retirees

- Whole Foods Focus: Eating whole, minimally processed foods provides your body with essential nutrients. Incorporate plenty of fruits, vegetables, lean proteins like chicken or beans, and whole grains such as brown rice or oatmeal.

- Hydration: As we age, our sense of thirst diminishes, making it easy to become dehydrated. Be sure to drink water regularly, aiming for around 8 glasses a day.

- Portion Control: Watch your portion sizes to prevent overeating, especially since our metabolism tends to slow down with age. Eating smaller, frequent meals can keep your energy levels consistent throughout the day.

- Nutrient-Rich Foods: Prioritize foods high in vitamins and minerals, such as dark leafy greens, berries, and nuts, to support heart health, vision, and bone strength.

Mental Wellness: Staying Sharp and Engaged

Retirement offers the chance to relax, but it's also a time to engage your brain in new and exciting ways. Staying mentally sharp is essential for preventing cognitive decline and keeping yourself feeling fulfilled and purposeful.

Mental Stimulation Is Key

Your brain needs as much exercise as your body. Regular mental challenges can delay cognitive decline, sharpen your memory, and improve your problem-solving skills. Take Mary, for example. After retiring, she decided to pursue a passion she had always put on the back burner—learning to paint. She found that focusing on the intricacies of painting improved her concentration and gave her a creative outlet that kept her feeling young and sharp.

Practical Tips for Staying Mentally Sharp

- Learning New Skills: The brain thrives on novelty. Pick up a new skill or hobby like photography, cooking, or even learning a new language. Engaging in lifelong learning keeps your mind active and alert.

- Games and Puzzles: Games like Sudoku, crossword puzzles, and chess are fun ways to keep your brain working. They stimulate your mind, improve memory, and promote critical thinking.

- Stay Curious: Read books, watch documentaries, or take online courses. You can explore new topics you never had time to study during your working years.

- Mindfulness Practices: Practicing mindfulness or meditation can help improve your focus, reduce stress, and promote mental clarity. Simple daily breathing exercises or guided meditation sessions can work wonders for mental well-being.

Staying Social for Mental Health

Mental wellness is strongly connected to your social life. Maintaining strong social connections not only provides emotional support but also helps keep your mind stimulated. Engaging in conversations, meeting new people, and sharing experiences are all forms of mental exercise.

Building and Maintaining a Social Network

Social interaction is one of the most important—and enjoyable—parts of retirement. Maintaining relationships and building new social networks can greatly enhance your emotional and physical health, and even increase longevity.

Why Social Connections Matter

Humans are inherently social creatures. Being socially connected can reduce feelings of loneliness, depression, and anxiety, which are more common in older adults. Let's look at Carol, a widow in her late 60s. After her husband passed away, she felt isolated and disconnected. But after joining a local gardening club, Carol found herself surrounded by a supportive community, made new friends, and rediscovered her love for the outdoors. Social interaction, she says, "brought color back into my life."

Practical Ways to Build and Maintain a Social Network

- Reconnect with Family and Friends: Retirement gives you more time to connect with family and old friends. Make a point to reach out, set up regular phone or video calls, or schedule in-person visits.

- Join Clubs or Groups: Explore clubs or organizations that match your interests, whether it's hiking, painting, book clubs, or community service. These groups not only keep you engaged but also provide a steady social outlet.

- Volunteer: Volunteering is a great way to meet new people and give back to your community. Whether it's tutoring, helping at a food bank, or working with animals, volunteering keeps you connected and purposeful.

- Technology for Connection: Don't be afraid of technology. Learning to use video calls, social media, and messaging apps can help you stay in touch with distant family members and friends. Virtual game nights or book clubs can bring people together from all over the world.

Conclusion

Staying active and healthy in retirement goes beyond just keeping fit—it involves nurturing your body, mind, and social life. Whether you're taking up new hobbies, joining social groups, or improving your nutrition, each step you take contributes to a happier and more fulfilling retirement. Embrace this time as an opportunity to not only rest but to grow in new directions, maintaining your health and joy in the years ahead.

Chapter 8

Navigating the Emotional Transition to Retirement

Retirement is often seen as a long-awaited reward for decades of hard work. Yet, for many, the emotional and psychological journey into this next phase of life can be surprisingly complex. This chapter explores how to cope with the inevitable changes to identity, find renewed purpose, and maintain mental and emotional well-being as you embrace your golden years.

Coping with Identity Changes Post-Career

For decades, your job or career has been a central part of your identity. Whether you were a teacher, engineer, entrepreneur, or manager, your profession shaped your self-perception, provided structure, and offered a sense of purpose. But when retirement begins, the sudden absence of work responsibilities can lead to feelings of disorientation or a loss of self-worth.

Why does this happen?

A career provides more than just income; it offers a sense of being needed, clear goals, and a structured routine. When that structure vanishes, it's natural to feel adrift. Many retirees find themselves grappling with questions like, "Who am I without my job?" and "What is my purpose now?"

What can help?

The first step in managing these identity changes is to acknowledge the emotional impact. It's perfectly normal to grieve the loss of a familiar role. Take time to reflect on the skills, talents, and knowledge you developed over your career, and realize that these qualities still define you. Your professional title may be gone, but the experience, wisdom, and personal strengths remain.

Engage in activities that allow you to continue contributing in meaningful ways. This could involve volunteering, mentoring younger professionals, or exploring a long-forgotten passion. The key is to find new channels through which you can apply your strengths and feel fulfilled.

Interactive Tip:

Write down three aspects of your job that you loved. Was it collaborating with others, solving problems, or the sense of achievement? Now consider how you can translate those passions into new activities. If you enjoyed teamwork, for example, you might join a local community group or club to stay connected.

Finding Purpose and Passion in Your Golden Years

After years of chasing deadlines and achieving professional goals, the wide-open landscape of retirement can feel overwhelming. You're faced with the exciting but daunting question of, "What do I do with all this free time?" Finding purpose in this new chapter of life is essential for emotional well-being and fulfillment.

Why is purpose so important?

Research shows that having a sense of purpose not only improves mental health but also has physical benefits, such as lowering the risk of cognitive decline and even extending life expectancy. During retirement, finding purpose might mean reconnecting with hobbies, taking up new interests, or dedicating your time to causes you care about.

Exploring New Passions

Retirement is your chance to rediscover old passions or explore completely new interests. Did you always dream of learning to paint, play an instrument, or travel the world? This is the time to follow those dreams. Some retirees find joy in giving back through volunteer work or by mentoring the younger generation. Others delve into creative pursuits, such as writing, gardening, or photography.

Think of this time as an adventure. Rather than worrying about doing it "right," allow yourself the freedom to try new things and see what excites you. Retirement offers a unique opportunity to shape your days based on what brings you joy.

Interactive Tip:

List five activities or hobbies you've always wanted to explore. For each one, write a simple action step you can take to get started. For example, if you've always wanted to travel, you could research local travel groups or sketch out a dream itinerary.

Rediscovering Passion Through Community

It's often easier to discover purpose when you're surrounded by like-minded individuals. Whether through joining clubs, attending workshops, or engaging in group activities, connecting with others who share your interests can deepen your sense of fulfillment. These new social circles offer support, companionship, and a renewed sense of belonging.

Strategies for Maintaining Mental and Emotional Health

While retirement can be liberating, it also comes with emotional and mental challenges. Adjusting to the newfound freedom, managing potential isolation, and keeping a healthy routine are all important aspects of staying emotionally balanced during this transition.

Embracing Change with Positivity

Retirement brings significant changes, but how you approach them matters. Instead of focusing on what's lost—like your job or structured routine—try to see this phase as an opportunity for growth. Embrace the positive aspects of aging, such as increased wisdom and the freedom to explore new interests. A positive mindset can help you see this time as one of personal reinvention rather than decline.

Staying Socially Connected

One of the biggest challenges retirees face is social isolation. Without the built-in interactions of a workplace, feelings of loneliness can creep in. Combat this by nurturing your relationships. Make an effort to stay connected with family and friends, and don't hesitate to form new bonds by joining social groups, clubs, or classes that interest you.

Interactive Tip:

Identify five people you'd like to reconnect with or deepen your relationship with during retirement. Schedule a call, coffee date, or even a video chat with them over the next month. Regular social interaction is key to maintaining emotional well-being.

Keeping Your Mind Sharp

Your brain needs as much exercise as your body. Mental stimulation is crucial in retirement to prevent cognitive decline and keep your mind sharp. Whether it's solving puzzles, reading, learning a new language, or taking online classes, find activities that challenge your mind and keep you engaged.

Technology offers easy access to lifelong learning. You can take virtual courses in subjects ranging from history to music, or join discussion groups to stimulate intellectual conversations. Creative pursuits like painting, writing, or crafting can also stimulate your mind in new ways.

Physical and Mental Health Connection

Physical activity plays a huge role in mental health. Exercise boosts your mood by releasing endorphins, reduces stress, and can even improve sleep quality. Consider incorporating regular physical activity into your retirement routine, whether it's walking, yoga, swimming, or another activity you enjoy.

Creating New Routines

Without the structure of a workday, retirement can sometimes feel aimless. Establishing a new routine can bring back a sense of purpose and help you maintain mental clarity. Your new routine doesn't need to be rigid, but it should include a balance of activities that support your physical, mental, and emotional health.

Create a weekly schedule that includes activities like exercise, hobbies, social time, and self-care. By doing so, you give your day structure and ensure that you're engaging in meaningful activities that keep your mind and body healthy.

Interactive Tip:

Develop a "Retirement Routine." Write out a daily or weekly plan that includes time for physical activity, social interaction, learning, and relaxation. Incorporate at least one "new experience" each week, whether it's trying a new recipe, visiting a nearby park, or learning a new skill.

Conclusion: Embracing the Emotional Transition to Retirement

Retirement marks the beginning of a new chapter, and while the emotional transition can be challenging, it's also an opportunity for growth and fulfillment. By addressing the changes in your identity, exploring new passions, and focusing on your mental and emotional health, you can create a retirement experience that's rich in purpose and joy.

The key to navigating this phase is to stay open to new experiences, maintain social connections, and prioritize your well-being. Retirement is not an end but a beginning—a chance to live your life with renewed purpose, surrounded by meaningful relationships and exciting opportunities.

Final Interactive Exercise:

Reflect on three things you want to achieve in retirement. These goals don't have to be grand—they can be as simple as spending more time with loved ones, traveling to new places, or learning a new skill. Write them down, and let these aspirations guide your journey through this next phase of life.

Chapter 9

Exploring Part-Time Work and Volunteer Opportunities

Retirement opens up a world of possibilities—a time to enjoy your freedom, pursue passions, and relax after years of work. However, for many, the prospect of completely stepping away from structure and activity can be challenging. Whether driven by a desire to stay engaged, supplement income, or give back to the community, retirees often find fulfillment in part-time work, volunteering, or turning hobbies into income streams. This chapter dives deep into the various ways you can remain active and purposeful in retirement, exploring part-time employment, meaningful volunteer opportunities, and ways to monetize your passions.

The Benefits of Part-Time Employment in Retirement

At first glance, retirement may seem like an endless vacation—no early mornings, no deadlines, and no office politics. But for many retirees, the initial excitement can give way to a sense of restlessness. The lack of structure, mental stimulation, and daily goals can leave you feeling adrift. Part-time employment can provide the perfect solution, allowing you to maintain a sense of purpose while enjoying the flexibility that retirement offers.

Why Consider Part-Time Work?

Part-time work in retirement offers a wide range of benefits beyond the financial aspect. While it's true that working a few hours each week can help supplement your retirement income, the rewards extend much further. Many retirees find that part-time employment offers a renewed sense of purpose, structure, and social interaction. Staying engaged in the workforce—whether through consulting, retail, or even a completely new field—can combat feelings of boredom and loneliness.

Financially, part-time work provides an additional safety net. Even with careful planning, retirement can bring unexpected expenses. The rising cost of healthcare, inflation, or sudden financial needs can put pressure on your savings. A flexible job can provide extra income without the demands of full-time work. Whether you need the money for necessities or just want to pad your travel or hobby budget, part-time work offers practical benefits.

Flexibility and Freedom

One of the most appealing aspects of part-time work is the freedom it provides. Unlike a full-time career, you have the ability to choose how much you want to work and where. Many retirees take the opportunity to explore jobs in industries they've always been curious about. Have you ever wanted to work at a bookstore, become a tour guide, or consult in your area of expertise? Part-time jobs give you the flexibility to explore new interests without the burden of a 40-hour workweek.

Part-time roles can be as casual or structured as you want them to be. You might choose seasonal work, freelance gigs, or even remote positions that allow you to work from the comfort of your home. With countless options available, part-time employment allows you to balance leisure and productivity on your own terms.

Mental and Emotional Benefits

In addition to the financial perks, part-time work offers significant psychological and emotional benefits. Engaging in meaningful tasks, interacting with colleagues, and having a routine can stave off the sense of aimlessness that some retirees experience. It also keeps your mind sharp, offering mental stimulation that challenges your brain in ways similar to your pre-retirement work life.

Studies have shown that retirees who engage in regular, mentally stimulating activities tend to experience lower rates of cognitive decline. Whether you're solving problems at work, learning new skills, or staying socially connected, part-time employment helps maintain cognitive health while offering fulfillment.

Practical Examination:

Evaluate your past career experience and compile a list of skills and interests you've developed. Research part-time jobs in industries that align with these skills and see how they match your desired level of flexibility. Write down three positions that interest you, noting their benefits, and think through how you would apply your talents to succeed in these roles.

Finding Meaningful Volunteer Work

Volunteering is another avenue for retirees to stay active, engaged, and connected to their community. Many people view retirement as a time to give back—an opportunity to use their skills, time, and energy for causes that matter to them. Whether you're passionate about education, social justice, the environment, or healthcare, volunteering allows you to contribute in ways that have a direct impact on the world around you.

The Emotional Rewards of Volunteering

Volunteering provides more than just the satisfaction of helping others—it has profound personal benefits as well. By giving your time and talents, you're engaging in work that aligns with your values, making the experience deeply rewarding. Studies have shown that volunteering can improve mental health, lower stress levels, and boost overall happiness. The act of giving back fosters a sense of purpose, which is crucial for mental well-being, especially in retirement.

Moreover, volunteering can create a sense of community. Retirees who volunteer regularly often build strong social networks with like-minded individuals, creating meaningful friendships. Whether you're volunteering at a local school, food bank, or community center, these connections can help combat feelings of loneliness and isolation that some retirees experience.

How to Find the Right Volunteer Opportunity

Finding the right volunteer opportunity begins with reflecting on your values, passions, and skills. Are you passionate about helping children succeed in school? Mentoring or tutoring may be a good fit. Do you care about environmental conservation? Look for community gardening projects, tree-planting events, or local wildlife organizations. The possibilities are vast, and there's likely a cause that aligns perfectly with your interests.

Many online platforms, such as VolunteerMatch or Idealist, allow you to search for volunteer opportunities based on location, interests, and skills. Local nonprofits, hospitals, animal shelters, and religious organizations are often in need of volunteers and can provide meaningful ways to give back. Even if you're not sure where to start, reaching out to organizations you admire can open doors to opportunities you may not have considered.

Practical Examination:

Consider your passions and identify three local organizations or causes that reflect your interests. Research their needs, and if possible, contact them to inquire about their volunteer opportunities. Create a comparison of what each organization offers, evaluating the time commitment, types of tasks, and personal satisfaction you could gain from each role. Decide which opportunity feels most rewarding to pursue.

Turning Hobbies into Income Streams

Retirement offers the perfect chance to dedicate more time to hobbies and interests you've always enjoyed. But what if those hobbies could become a source of income? Whether it's knitting, photography, writing, or woodworking, turning your passion into a business can provide both personal fulfillment and financial rewards.

Why Monetize Your Hobbies?

The idea of monetizing a hobby might sound daunting, but it doesn't have to feel like work. In fact, turning your passion into profit can enhance your sense of purpose and provide a creative outlet. You already love what you're doing, so why not share it with others and earn money in the process?

From selling handmade crafts on Etsy to offering photography services for events, there are countless ways to turn your talents into income. Not only does this provide financial benefits, but it also allows you to continue doing something you love, keeping you engaged and motivated.

Steps to Turn Your Hobby into an Income Stream

Start by assessing the market for your hobby. Is there a demand for your products or services? Whether you're creating art, writing blogs, or growing organic produce, there's likely a market out there for what you offer. Research how others in your field are selling their work and identify what makes your offerings unique.

Once you've established a potential market, begin small. You don't need to launch a full-scale business overnight. Start with small goals—perhaps listing a few items on an online marketplace, setting up a website, or offering your services to friends and family. As you grow more comfortable, you can expand your offerings, build a brand, and potentially turn your hobby into a steady income stream.

Practical Examination:

Pick a hobby you are passionate about and research three platforms or marketplaces where you could sell your products or services. Analyze each platform's audience, fees, and the ease of setting up a shop or profile. Create a basic plan outlining the first steps to start selling, such as creating sample products, building a portfolio, or launching a small online shop.

Wrapping It All Up: Finding Balance in Retirement

Whether through part-time work, volunteering, or monetizing hobbies, there are countless ways to make your retirement fulfilling, purposeful, and enjoyable. The beauty of retirement is that you're in control. You get to choose what excites you, what challenges you, and what gives your life meaning. These activities can enrich your retirement experience, providing structure, connection, and a sense of purpose.

Remember, the key to a happy retirement isn't filling every moment with obligations but finding balance. Whether you pursue part-time work, volunteer your time, or turn a passion into an income stream, the goal is to stay engaged in ways that bring joy and fulfillment. Explore the opportunities that interest you, be open to new experiences, and allow yourself the freedom to embrace the activities that resonate with you.

Final Practical Examination:
Take a moment to assess the different paths you could take—whether part-time work, volunteering, or turning a hobby into an income stream. Write down the key areas that interest you most and create a clear plan for how you'll begin exploring one of these opportunities. Outline the steps you need to take, the resources you'll need to gather, and a timeline for action. Then, take that first step toward creating a retirement that is both purposeful and rewarding.

Chapter 10

Traveling in Retirement: Planning and Budgeting

Retirement often sparks dreams of travel—whether it's exploring new cultures, visiting loved ones, or ticking off that long-awaited bucket list. But how do you make the most of your retirement travel while managing finances, health, and logistics? In this chapter, we'll cover practical strategies for planning trips, tips for traveling on a budget, considerations for long-term stays abroad, and essential health and travel insurance options. Retirement is the perfect time to enjoy new experiences, and with proper planning, you can travel with confidence and ease.

Budget-Friendly Travel Tips and Destinations

Travel in retirement doesn't have to break the bank. With some savvy planning, you can stretch your travel dollars and still enjoy memorable adventures. Here are some practical tips to help you get the most value from your trips:

1. Travel During the Off-Season

One of the biggest advantages of retirement travel is the flexibility to travel during off-peak seasons. By avoiding high-traffic times like school vacations and holidays, you can save significantly on flights, accommodations, and activities. For example, visiting Europe in the spring or fall can offer beautiful weather without the crowds or peak prices. Similarly, tropical destinations like the Caribbean often have shoulder seasons with lower prices, but still offer great experiences.

2. Take Advantage of Senior Discounts

Many travel companies, including airlines, hotels, and tour operators, offer special rates for seniors. Always ask about discounts for retirees when booking transportation, accommodations, or activities. Sites like AARP Travel or Senior Nomads also offer exclusive deals tailored for older travelers.

3. Consider House-Sitting or Home Exchanges

One way to save on accommodations is through house-sitting or home exchange programs. These allow you to stay in someone's home for free, often in exchange for taking care of their property while they're away. Platforms like TrustedHousesitters or HomeExchange offer listings all over the world, giving you the chance to experience a destination like a local while significantly reducing your accommodation costs.

4. Plan Group Travel or Tours

Traveling with a group of friends or fellow retirees can lead to group discounts and shared costs for accommodations and transportation. Group tours, especially those designed for older travelers, often bundle flights, hotels, and activities at a lower rate. Plus, traveling in a group provides built-in companionship and safety, particularly in unfamiliar destinations.

5. Explore Budget-Friendly Destinations

Some destinations are known for being more affordable than others while still offering rich cultural experiences. Countries in Southeast Asia, such as Thailand or Vietnam, offer excellent value for retirees, with low-cost food, accommodations, and transportation. Closer to home, places like Mexico and Portugal also provide affordable living costs for retirees looking to stretch their travel budget while enjoying a high quality of life.

Practical Exercise:

Create a list of five destinations you've always wanted to visit. Research off-peak travel times for each location and see how much you can save by traveling during less crowded months. Compare flight prices, accommodations, and senior discounts to see which destination offers the best value.

Long-Term Travel and Living Abroad: Pros and Cons

For many retirees, the idea of spending extended periods abroad or even living in another country is appealing. Whether you're considering long-term travel or relocating abroad, it's important to weigh the pros and cons to ensure it's the right fit for your lifestyle and financial situation.

Pros of Long-Term Travel and Living Abroad

1. New Experiences and Cultural Immersion

One of the most exciting aspects of long-term travel or living abroad is the opportunity to fully immerse yourself in a new culture. Living like a local, learning a new language, and developing connections with people from different backgrounds can enrich your life and provide personal growth.

2. Lower Cost of Living in Some Countries

Many retirees choose to live abroad because of the lower cost of living in countries like Mexico, Costa Rica, or Spain. You may find that your retirement savings stretch further in these countries, allowing you to live comfortably on a budget that might be restrictive at home.

3. Better Weather and Lifestyle

For retirees looking to escape harsh winters or enjoy a more relaxed pace of life, living abroad in warmer climates or slower-paced regions can offer an improved quality of life. Whether it's sunny beaches or scenic mountain villages, you can choose a location that matches your desired lifestyle.

4. Potential Tax Benefits

In some cases, retirees living abroad may qualify for favorable tax treatment, especially if their income comes from pensions or investments. It's important to consult a tax advisor to understand how living abroad will impact your tax obligations.

Cons of Long-Term Travel and Living Abroad

1. Healthcare Access and Quality

One of the biggest concerns for retirees living abroad is access to healthcare. While some countries offer affordable, high-quality healthcare, others may have limited services, particularly in rural or remote areas. It's essential to research the healthcare system in your chosen country and ensure that it meets your needs.

2. Legal and Residency Requirements

Living abroad requires navigating local residency laws, visas, and work permits. Some countries have specific residency programs for retirees, but these often come with minimum income or investment requirements. Understanding these legal processes can be complex and may require assistance from a legal advisor.

3. Social Isolation and Cultural Differences

While living abroad offers many new experiences, it can also be challenging, especially if you don't speak the language fluently or if cultural differences are significant. Some retirees struggle with homesickness or feelings of isolation, particularly if they're far from family and friends.

4. Managing Finances and Taxes Across Borders

Retirees living abroad must manage their finances in multiple currencies and navigate tax obligations both in their home country and their new country of residence. It's crucial to work with financial advisors familiar with international tax laws and banking practices to avoid any pitfalls.

Practical Exercise:

Make a list of potential countries where you'd like to live or spend extended time. For each country, research the cost of living, healthcare options, and residency requirements. Compare the pros and cons to see which destination aligns best with your financial, health, and lifestyle needs.

Health and Travel Insurance for Retirees

Traveling in retirement is exciting, but it's essential to make sure you're adequately protected, particularly when it comes to health and travel insurance. Here's what retirees should know about staying covered while traveling, whether for short trips or extended stays abroad.

1. Medicare and Travel

If you're a U.S. retiree, it's important to know that Medicare generally does not cover healthcare services outside of the United States. This means you'll need additional coverage for any medical emergencies that occur while you're traveling. Supplemental plans, such as Medigap or Medicare Advantage, may offer some limited coverage for foreign travel, but it's essential to review your plan and understand any restrictions.

2. Travel Insurance for Short-Term Trips

For short trips, purchasing travel insurance can provide coverage for medical emergencies, trip cancellations, lost luggage, and more. Travel insurance policies can be customized to meet your needs, and many insurers offer specific plans for seniors or retirees. Be sure to choose a policy that includes adequate medical coverage, especially if you're traveling to countries with high healthcare costs.

3. International Health Insurance for Long-Term Travel or Living Abroad

If you're planning to live abroad or travel for extended periods, consider purchasing international health insurance. This type of coverage is designed for expatriates and provides access to medical care worldwide. International health insurance typically covers hospital stays, surgeries, doctor visits, and sometimes even routine checkups. Be sure to choose a plan that covers pre-existing conditions if applicable.

4. Evacuation and Repatriation Insurance

In the event of a serious medical emergency, some travel insurance policies offer evacuation and repatriation services. This means that if you need specialized treatment that isn't available in your current location, the insurance company will cover the cost of transporting you to the nearest suitable hospital or even back to your home country for treatment. This coverage is particularly important if you're traveling to remote areas or countries with limited medical facilities.

5. Understanding Coverage Limits and Exclusions

When selecting health or travel insurance, it's important to read the fine print and understand what's covered—and what's not. Some policies exclude coverage for high-risk activities like scuba diving or skiing, while others may have age limits or restrictions on pre-existing conditions. Make sure to choose a plan that fits your travel itinerary and medical needs.

Practical Exercise:

Review your current health insurance coverage and identify any gaps in coverage for international travel. Research supplemental travel or international health insurance plans that align with your travel goals, and compare the benefits and costs of different policies. Choose a plan that provides comprehensive coverage, including medical emergencies, evacuations, and trip cancellations.

Wrapping Up

Traveling in retirement can be an exciting and fulfilling way to explore the world, meet new people, and experience different cultures. By planning carefully, budgeting wisely, and ensuring proper health and travel insurance, you can enjoy your travels with peace of mind. Whether you're embarking on short getaways, long-term adventures, or even living abroad, retirement offers the freedom to make travel dreams a reality.

Chapter 11

Preparing for the Unexpected

Retirement is a time to relax and enjoy the fruits of your years of hard work. However, life is full of surprises, and even the most meticulously planned retirement can be met with unforeseen challenges. These may include financial hurdles like market downturns, unexpected health issues, or even family responsibilities. Being prepared for these surprises is key to maintaining financial stability and peace of mind in your golden years.

In this chapter, we will explore how to build a solid emergency fund, manage market volatility, and adapt your retirement plan to life's inevitable changes. By planning ahead and staying flexible, you'll be able to face whatever comes your way with confidence.

Emergency Funds: How Much Should You Save?

One of the most important pillars of a secure retirement is having an emergency fund. This fund acts as a buffer against unplanned expenses, such as medical bills, home repairs, or other unexpected financial surprises. But the key question is: How much should you save?

Why an Emergency Fund is Critical in Retirement

During your working years, you likely relied on your paycheck to cover unexpected expenses. In retirement, your income may come from fixed sources such as Social Security, pensions, or withdrawals from your retirement accounts. Without a regular paycheck, unplanned expenses can throw your financial plan off balance. Having an emergency fund ensures you don't need to withdraw from your retirement accounts unexpectedly, which could have negative tax consequences or disrupt your long-term investment strategy.

How Much Should You Save?

The rule of thumb for an emergency fund is typically 3 to 6 months' worth of living expenses, but for retirees, it's advisable to aim for a larger cushion—6 to 12 months of expenses. Why? In retirement, emergencies like health problems, home repairs, or sudden travel needs can arise, and you may not have the same income flexibility as before. Let's break it down:

- Health-related costs: Even with Medicare or supplemental insurance, out-of-pocket medical costs can be significant. Medical emergencies, surgeries, or long-term care can strain your budget.

- Home and vehicle repairs: Aging homes and cars often require expensive maintenance, from replacing a roof to fixing a broken HVAC system or car repairs.

- Unexpected travel or family emergencies: A family crisis, such as the need to care for a loved one, may require unplanned and often costly travel.

Where Should You Keep Your Emergency Fund?

An emergency fund should be easily accessible and secure, but it should also be in a low-risk account where it can earn some interest. High-yield savings accounts, money market accounts, and short-term certificates of deposit (CDs) are good options. These allow your emergency fund to grow modestly while remaining liquid for immediate needs.

Practical Exercise:

Calculate your monthly expenses, including mortgage or rent, utilities, groceries, healthcare, and entertainment. Multiply that amount by 6 to 12 months to determine how much you need to save in your emergency fund. Evaluate your current savings and create a plan to reach your target amount if you haven't already.

Dealing with Market Volatility and Economic Downturns

The stock market can be unpredictable, and even retirees who rely on a diversified portfolio for income can feel the stress of market volatility. Preparing for these fluctuations—while maintaining a long-term perspective—helps protect your financial security in retirement.

Understanding Market Volatility

Markets naturally go through cycles of growth and contraction. While this is normal, it can be unsettling if you're relying on your investments for income. Retirement typically comes with a desire for stability, but fluctuations in the stock market are inevitable. Understanding that volatility is part of the market's behavior can help you avoid panic when downturns occur.

What Should You Do During a Market Downturn?

It's natural to feel the urge to sell investments during a market downturn to prevent further losses. However, selling at the wrong time can lock in those losses and reduce your ability to recover when the market bounces back. Here are some key strategies for managing market volatility:

1. Stick to Your Plan: If your retirement plan is built around diversified investments, trust the process. Diversification helps reduce the risk of losing too much in any single asset class.

2. Use Cash Reserves: In periods of market downturns, avoid selling investments at a loss by using your emergency fund or cash savings to cover living expenses.

3. Rebalance Your Portfolio: Market changes can cause your portfolio's allocation to shift. Periodically rebalancing your portfolio ensures that it stays aligned with your risk tolerance and long-term goals.

Managing Inflation Risk

Another important factor to consider in retirement is inflation. Rising prices can erode your purchasing power, making it harder to cover living expenses as the years go by. Here are a few strategies to help manage inflation risk:

- Invest in Treasury Inflation-Protected Securities (TIPS): These government bonds are designed to keep pace with inflation, offering protection against rising costs.

- Consider Dividend-Paying Stocks: These stocks can provide a growing income stream that helps offset inflation.

- Maintain Some Exposure to Stocks: Even in retirement, having some stock exposure can help your portfolio grow, outpacing inflation over time.

Practical Exercise:

Review your investment portfolio and evaluate how well diversified it is across asset classes like stocks, bonds, and cash. If needed, consult with a financial advisor to assess your portfolio's resilience in the face of market volatility and inflation. Ensure it aligns with your risk tolerance and long-term goals.

Adapting Your Retirement Plan to Life's Changes

Retirement rarely follows a straight path. Whether it's health changes, unexpected family responsibilities, or shifting lifestyle goals, being flexible and adapting your financial plan to life's changes is essential for a secure and fulfilling retirement.

1. Health Changes and Medical Expenses

As you age, healthcare becomes an increasingly important part of your financial plan. Unexpected illnesses, injuries, or even the need for long-term care can dramatically impact your budget and lifestyle. Proactively planning for health changes helps ensure you're financially prepared.

- Stay Proactive About Health Insurance: Regularly review your Medicare or private health insurance coverage to ensure it meets your needs. If necessary, consider adding supplemental insurance to cover gaps.

- Consider Long-Term Care Insurance: Long-term care can be expensive, and many retirees are unprepared for these costs. Long-term care insurance helps cover expenses like nursing home stays or in-home care.

- Create a Health Directive and Power of Attorney: Ensure your healthcare wishes are respected by establishing advance directives and assigning someone trusted to make decisions on your behalf if needed.

2. Family Responsibilities

Many retirees find themselves taking on new family responsibilities, such as caring for grandchildren or supporting aging parents. These obligations can add emotional and financial strain, so it's crucial to incorporate them into your retirement plan.

- Set Boundaries with Family Support: While it's natural to want to help family members, be mindful of your own financial limits. Have honest discussions about what level of support you can provide without jeopardizing your retirement.

- Factor Family Support into Your Budget: If you anticipate ongoing financial support for a family member, adjust your budget accordingly to ensure you can meet their needs without impacting your own security.

3. Changes in Lifestyle or Goals

Over time, your vision for retirement may change. Whether you decide to travel more, pick up a new hobby, or downsize to a simpler lifestyle, adapting your financial plan to your evolving goals is key.

- Reevaluate Your Spending Habits: As your priorities shift, take a fresh look at your budget. You may need to adjust your spending to reflect your new interests or goals.

- Adjust Withdrawal Rates if Needed: If your expenses rise or fall significantly, consider adjusting your retirement account withdrawal rates to ensure your savings last as long as you need them.

Practical Exercise:

Think about possible life scenarios that could impact your retirement—such as health issues, new family responsibilities, or evolving personal goals. Write down a list of these scenarios and how you might adapt your financial plan to accommodate each one. Ensure that your budget, insurance coverage, and estate plans remain current and flexible.

Wrapping Up

Retirement is an exciting phase of life, full of opportunities for relaxation, exploration, and fulfillment. However, it's essential to be prepared for life's inevitable surprises. By building a robust emergency fund, managing market volatility, and staying flexible with your plans, you'll be well-equipped to navigate the unexpected and protect your financial future.

With the right strategies in place, you can confidently enjoy your retirement knowing you're ready for whatever comes your way. Flexibility, preparation, and regular financial check-ins will help ensure that your retirement remains secure, stable, and filled with peace of mind.

Chapter 12

The Role of Family in Retirement Planning

Retirement isn't just a personal milestone; it often involves the family in ways you might not initially expect. From financial support for adult children to caregiving responsibilities, family dynamics play a critical role in shaping your retirement experience. Open communication, thoughtful planning, and setting boundaries are essential to balancing your own needs with those of your loved ones. In this chapter, we'll explore how to have productive discussions with family members about your retirement plans, the challenges of providing financial support to adult children, and the possibility of becoming a caregiver. Together, these insights will help you navigate family relationships and responsibilities while safeguarding your retirement goals.

Discussing Your Plans with Family Members

Retirement marks a significant life transition, not just for you but for your family as well. Your decisions about where to live, how you'll manage your finances, and what kind of support you might need can impact those around you. Open and honest communication with family members about your plans is essential for managing expectations and preventing misunderstandings.

Why It's Important to Discuss Retirement Plans

Retirement often involves changes that affect more than just the retiree. You might be thinking about downsizing, relocating, or cutting back on financial contributions to family members. Without clear communication, these decisions can lead to confusion or even tension. Having these conversations early allows everyone to understand your goals and how they might fit into them.

- Managing Expectations: Family members may have assumptions about your retirement. For example, they might expect you to stay nearby, continue providing financial support, or be available to help with grandchildren. Being upfront about your intentions can prevent disappointment or unrealistic expectations later.

- Reducing Pressure: Some retirees feel obligated to stay close to family or continue supporting them financially. Being clear about your own desires—whether that's pursuing hobbies, traveling, or downsizing—can help relieve pressure on both sides.

- Clarifying Health and Care Preferences: As you age, it's important that your family understands your health-related wishes, including end-of-life care. Discuss your advance directives, living will, or healthcare power of attorney so your loved ones are prepared if the need arises.

How to Approach the Conversation

Talking about your retirement plans doesn't have to be a formal or intimidating process, but it should be thoughtful. Here are some tips for making the conversation productive and positive:

- Pick the Right Time: Timing is key. Make sure you choose a moment when everyone can be focused and calm. Family gatherings or scheduled meetings can work well for this type of discussion.

- Be Open and Positive: Frame your retirement plans in a positive light. Share your excitement about what's ahead and invite your family to ask questions or share concerns. This helps make the conversation feel collaborative rather than confrontational.

- Encourage Dialogue: Encourage family members to share their thoughts and feelings. They may have insights or questions you hadn't considered, and involving them in the process makes them feel valued and respected.

Example of a Family Conversation:

- "I've been thinking a lot about what I want my retirement to look like. I'm considering moving to a smaller home in a different city. I'd love to hear how you feel about this and whether there are any concerns or thoughts you'd like to share."

Practical Tip:

Make a list of topics you want to discuss with your family, such as your living arrangements, financial plans, and health directives. Prepare to share your thoughts openly, but also be ready to listen to their feedback. These conversations should be two-way dialogues, fostering understanding and support.

Navigating Financial Support for Adult Children

A common challenge in retirement is deciding how to manage financial support for adult children. Whether it's helping with a home down payment, paying for education, or offering temporary assistance during hard times, providing financial help can be both rewarding and risky. It's crucial to find a balance that allows you to help your children without compromising your own financial security.

Balancing Family Support and Financial Security

Retirees often face pressure to help their adult children financially, especially if they have the means to do so. However, providing too much assistance can strain your retirement savings and prevent you from fully enjoying your golden years. Before offering support, consider the long-term impact on your finances.

- Evaluating the Impact: Helping adult children financially may seem manageable, but repeated contributions can quickly add up. Whether it's covering monthly expenses or offering lump sums, you need to calculate how these decisions will affect your overall retirement plan.

- Setting Limits: Even if your children are struggling financially, it's important to establish boundaries around how much support you can provide. Remember, your retirement savings are finite, and once depleted, they may be difficult to replace.

- Encouraging Financial Independence: While it's natural to want to help, too much financial support can undermine your children's ability to manage their own finances. Rather than offering long-term financial help, consider providing resources or advice that empowers them to become more self-reliant.

Setting Boundaries and Communicating Clearly

When it comes to helping adult children, clear communication and defined limits are essential. It's important that your children understand what you're willing to offer—and when that help will end.

- Be Honest About Your Financial Situation: If you need to limit financial support to protect your retirement, let your children know. They may not realize the strain their requests place on your finances.

- Establish a Timeframe or Budget: If you're offering financial help, consider setting a specific dollar amount or timeframe for support. This ensures you don't become a long-term safety net at the expense of your own security.

- Provide Non-Monetary Assistance: Instead of giving money directly, offer to help with budgeting, career advice, or debt management strategies. Teaching your children financial literacy can have a longer-lasting impact than a one-time financial gift.

Example of Setting Boundaries:

- "We understand that you're going through a tough financial period, and we want to help where we can. However, we also need to make sure our own retirement savings are secure. Let's discuss how we can assist you now and help you plan for the future."

Practical Tip:

Develop a clear financial plan for any assistance you provide to your adult children. Decide in advance how much you're willing to contribute and communicate these boundaries. This ensures that your retirement savings remain intact and that your children know what to expect.

Preparing for the Possibility of Becoming a Caregiver

As people live longer, more retirees find themselves taking on caregiving responsibilities for aging parents, a spouse, or even other relatives. While caregiving can be a fulfilling role, it's also physically, emotionally, and financially demanding. Preparing for the possibility of becoming a caregiver can help minimize its impact on your retirement plans.

Understanding the Demands of Caregiving

Caregiving often comes with unexpected responsibilities, from helping with day-to-day activities to managing medical care. This role can be both rewarding and exhausting, and it's essential to consider how caregiving could affect your lifestyle and financial plans.

- Financial Costs: Caregiving can be expensive, especially if medical equipment, home modifications, or in-home care services are required. These costs can quickly add up, affecting your retirement budget.

- Time Commitment: Depending on the level of care needed, caregiving can become a full-time job. This can interfere with your own plans for travel, hobbies, or even maintaining your social connections in retirement.

- Physical and Emotional Toll: Caring for a loved one can be physically demanding and emotionally draining. Burnout is a common issue among caregivers, especially if they lack adequate support.

Planning Ahead for Caregiving

If you anticipate taking on a caregiving role, it's crucial to plan ahead. This not only ensures that your loved one gets the care they need but also helps protect your retirement lifestyle and finances.

- Discuss Caregiving Responsibilities with Family: If caregiving is likely, have open discussions with family members about how responsibilities will be shared. You may not need to shoulder the burden alone; other relatives might be able to contribute time, money, or support.

- Consider Long-Term Care Insurance: Long-term care insurance can help cover the cost of in-home care, assisted living, or nursing home care. This type of coverage can significantly ease the financial strain on both you and your family.

- Utilize Professional Services: It's important to recognize when professional help is needed. Hiring a part-time caregiver or using respite services can give you a much-needed break and ensure your loved one receives the best possible care.

Example of Planning for Caregiving:

- "We need to start planning for the possibility that Dad might need more help as he gets older. Let's talk about how we'll manage this as a family and what resources we might need."

Practical Tip:

Research local caregiving resources, such as support groups, respite care programs, and financial assistance for caregivers. Knowing what's available can help you manage caregiving responsibilities more effectively and prevent burnout.

Wrapping Up

Family plays a central role in retirement planning. Whether it's discussing your retirement goals with loved ones, navigating financial support for adult children, or preparing for caregiving responsibilities, open communication and clear boundaries are essential for a smooth retirement. By planning ahead, setting limits, and remaining flexible, you can balance family needs with your own retirement goals, ensuring a fulfilling and financially secure future for both you and your loved ones.

Chapter 13

Leveraging Technology to Enhance Retirement

Retirement today looks very different from previous generations, largely thanks to technology. From managing your finances to staying connected with loved ones and picking up new skills, technology offers countless ways to make your retirement more enriching, convenient, and fulfilling. In this chapter, we'll explore how online tools can simplify financial management, ways to stay digitally connected with family and friends, and how technology can be a gateway to learning new skills and hobbies. Leveraging these tools will allow you to enhance your retirement experience in meaningful ways.

Online Tools for Managing Finances and Investments

One of the most critical aspects of retirement is managing your finances effectively to ensure your savings last as long as possible. Thanks to advances in technology, retirees now have access to a variety of online tools and platforms that make it easier to track spending, manage investments, and optimize financial decisions.

Budgeting and Expense Tracking

Maintaining a clear understanding of your day-to-day and long-term financial situation is key to a stress-free retirement. Online budgeting tools and apps help retirees keep a detailed record of expenses, manage monthly bills, and set spending goals.

- Apps like Mint and YNAB (You Need a Budget): These platforms allow you to connect your bank accounts, retirement funds, and credit cards in one place, providing a comprehensive overview of your finances. They categorize expenses, offer insights into spending patterns, and allow you to set savings goals.

- Simple Interfaces and Alerts: Many apps come with user-friendly dashboards and can send alerts when you're approaching a spending limit or when bills are due. This makes it easier to stay on top of your budget without the need for complex spreadsheets or manual calculations.

Investment Management

Whether you're new to investing or a seasoned investor, managing retirement investments can be daunting, especially with market fluctuations. Thankfully, online investment platforms can simplify the process, giving you more control over your portfolio.

- Robo-Advisors like Betterment or Wealthfront: These automated platforms help manage your investments based on your risk tolerance and goals. They offer portfolio management, tax optimization, and even retirement planning advice. You can monitor your investments in real-time and make adjustments when necessary.

- Tracking Investment Performance: Online tools like Personal Capital provide a detailed look at your overall portfolio, including your 401(k), IRAs, and other assets. They help track performance, analyze fees, and even offer tools to project how long your savings will last, allowing you to make informed decisions about withdrawals and investment strategies.

Online Banking and Payment Solutions

In addition to investment management, online banking has made day-to-day financial tasks much easier for retirees. With online banking, you can:

- Pay Bills Easily: Set up automatic payments for utilities, insurance, or other recurring bills, reducing the risk of missing a payment.

- Track Transactions and Statements: Keep track of your checking and savings account transactions in real-time from your phone or computer.

- Monitor Fraud and Security: Many banks offer fraud alerts and enhanced security features that protect your accounts from unauthorized activity. You can receive immediate notifications if anything suspicious occurs.

Practical Tip:

Explore online financial management tools and choose one that fits your needs. Start by linking your accounts to a budgeting app or a robo-advisor, and make a habit of checking in regularly to ensure you're meeting your financial goals.

Staying Connected with Family and Friends Digitally

For many retirees, staying connected with family and friends is a top priority, and technology has made this easier than ever. With social media platforms, video calls, and instant messaging apps, you can maintain close relationships, even if loved ones live far away. Digital communication offers a lifeline to emotional support, companionship, and social interaction.

Social Media and Messaging Platforms

Social media platforms such as Facebook, Instagram, and WhatsApp are fantastic for staying in touch with family, reconnecting with old friends, and sharing updates about your life. These tools allow you to remain involved in the lives of your children, grandchildren, and other relatives, even if you're not physically together.

- Facebook and Instagram: These platforms enable you to share photos, videos, and updates, helping you feel more connected to everyday moments. You can also join groups and communities that align with your hobbies or interests, allowing you to meet new people or find support.

- WhatsApp and Facebook Messenger: Messaging apps provide instant communication with family and friends, no matter where they are. You can send texts, voice messages, photos, and videos in real-time, making it easy to stay in touch.

Video Calls and Virtual Gatherings

For more intimate and personal communication, video calls through platforms like Zoom, Skype, or FaceTime have become incredibly popular. These tools allow face-to-face interaction, making it feel like you're in the same room, even if you're miles apart.

- Zoom and Skype: Perfect for virtual family gatherings, holiday celebrations, or casual catch-ups, video call platforms support group conversations. You can also organize virtual game nights or movie-watching parties, creating fun ways to stay connected.

- FaceTime or Google Duo: These mobile apps make one-on-one video calls simple and accessible for anyone with a smartphone. A quick FaceTime with a grandchild or close friend can instantly brighten your day.

Staying Connected Through Shared Activities

In addition to communication, technology offers opportunities to bond with family and friends through shared experiences. You can play games, share photos, and even watch TV shows or movies together using digital platforms.

- Shared Streaming Services: Apps like Netflix Party allow you to watch a show or movie with family members while chatting together in real-time. It's a great way to have a shared experience from the comfort of your own home.

- Online Games: Play interactive games like chess, Scrabble, or even trivia with family members online. This adds a layer of fun and friendly competition to your digital interactions.

Practical Tip:

Set up regular virtual meetings with your loved ones. Whether it's a weekly video call or a monthly movie night, having a digital routine can help keep relationships strong. Consider joining social media platforms or messaging apps to stay up-to-date with family and friends, especially if travel or distance makes frequent visits challenging.

Learning New Skills and Hobbies Through Technology

Retirement is the perfect time to pursue new interests, learn new skills, or revisit old hobbies that you may not have had time for during your working years. Technology has opened up vast possibilities for learning and personal growth, all from the comfort of your home.

Online Courses and Educational Platforms

If you've always wanted to learn something new, whether it's painting, photography, or even a foreign language, online learning platforms offer endless opportunities. Many of these courses are flexible, allowing you to learn at your own pace.

- Platforms like Coursera, Udemy, or MasterClass: These websites provide access to courses on a wide range of subjects, from history and literature to cooking and music. Many are taught by experts or professionals in the field, offering a high-quality educational experience.

- YouTube Tutorials: For those looking to dabble in a hobby or skill without the structure of a formal course, YouTube offers a wealth of free tutorials. Whether you're interested in woodworking, knitting, or learning how to garden, there's likely a step-by-step video available to guide you.

Expanding Your Tech Knowledge

For those who may not be familiar with new technologies, learning the basics of computers, smartphones, or tablets can be an incredibly empowering experience. Many online resources cater specifically to seniors who are new to digital tools.

- AARP and Senior Planet: Both platforms offer online workshops, tutorials, and guides designed to teach older adults how to navigate the digital world. You can find step-by-step instructions on everything from using social media to managing online banking.

Virtual Clubs and Online Communities

If you're passionate about a particular hobby, joining an online community can help you meet like-minded individuals and deepen your knowledge. Many retirees find fulfillment in participating in virtual clubs or discussion groups centered around shared interests.

- Book Clubs, Art Groups, and Music Forums: Virtual clubs on platforms like Goodreads or Reddit allow retirees to share their love of literature, art, or music with others from around the world. These forums often host discussions, challenges, and even live virtual events.

- Fitness Apps and Virtual Exercise Classes: Staying physically active is crucial in retirement, and technology has made it easier to access fitness resources. You can join live or recorded yoga classes, strength training, or even Tai Chi through apps like Peloton or YouTube.

Practical Tip:

Identify a new skill or hobby you've always wanted to explore and sign up for an online course or watch a few tutorials on YouTube. Look into virtual clubs or communities that match your interests and consider joining one. The sense of belonging and shared learning can make retirement even more rewarding.

Wrapping Up

Technology has revolutionized the way we experience retirement, offering tools and platforms that make managing finances, staying connected, and learning new skills easier than ever. By embracing these technological advancements, you can enhance your retirement experience, remain financially savvy, and maintain strong social connections, all while continuing to grow and learn in your golden years. Whether you're interested in exploring new hobbies, maintaining relationships, or staying in control of your finances, leveraging technology is a valuable way to ensure a fulfilling and active retirement.

Chapter 14

Final Steps to a Secure and Fulfilling Retirement

As you transition into retirement, the journey doesn't end with financial independence. Ensuring a secure and fulfilling retirement requires continuous reflection, adjustments, and embracing new opportunities. This chapter explores how to keep your retirement plan flexible, set new goals for yourself, celebrate milestones, and build a legacy that leaves a lasting impact. Whether you're just beginning retirement or have been enjoying it for years, taking these final steps will help you navigate this phase of life with purpose and fulfillment.

Regularly Reviewing and Adjusting Your Retirement Plan

Even though retirement may feel like a time to settle into a routine, life is still full of surprises. Market fluctuations, health issues, or unexpected opportunities can arise, making it essential to regularly review and adjust your retirement plan. Flexibility is key to ensuring your financial security throughout retirement.

Why Regular Reviews Are Important

Just because you've mapped out a retirement plan doesn't mean it will stay relevant forever. Life evolves, and so do your needs. Regularly reviewing your retirement plan ensures that it still aligns with your goals, lifestyle, and financial circumstances.

- Financial Changes: The value of investments can fluctuate due to market conditions, and inflation can affect the cost of living. Your income sources, such as Social Security or pension payments, may need reassessment to account for these changes.

- Health Considerations: As you age, healthcare needs can increase, and medical expenses may rise. Reviewing your insurance coverage, including Medicare or supplemental insurance, is essential to avoiding financial strain.

- Family Dynamics: Family changes, such as helping adult children, welcoming new grandchildren, or caregiving for a spouse, can shift your priorities and require adjustments to your budget and time management.

Steps to Keep Your Plan Current

- Annual Financial Check-ups: At least once a year, take time to go over your retirement plan. Review your spending patterns, income streams, and investment performance. Make sure your portfolio is still diversified and aligned with your risk tolerance.

- Assess Your Spending: Have your expenses changed since you first retired? Perhaps you're spending more on travel or healthcare than anticipated, or you're saving more than expected. Understanding your spending habits helps you stay on top of your finances and avoid running out of funds later in retirement.

- Seek Professional Guidance: If you're unsure how your retirement plan is faring, meeting with a financial advisor can provide insights into rebalancing your portfolio, managing withdrawals, and updating your plan to reflect current market conditions.

Practical Tip:

Set a reminder on your calendar for an annual financial review. Use this time to evaluate any changes in your retirement needs and make necessary adjustments to your investments, budget, or income sources. If significant life events have occurred, address them in your plan as well.

Setting New Goals and Celebrating Milestones

Retirement is a new chapter that allows you to pursue passions and goals you may have put on hold during your working years. While financial security is important, it's equally vital to set personal goals that provide meaning and excitement in your life. From learning new skills to traveling, volunteering, or pursuing a passion project, these goals can enrich your retirement.

The Importance of Goal Setting in Retirement

Many people enter retirement thinking it's a time to relax, but without structure or purpose, boredom or a sense of aimlessness can creep in. Setting new goals keeps you engaged, helps maintain mental and emotional well-being, and gives you a sense of accomplishment.

- Personal Growth: Retirement is an opportunity to pursue lifelong learning, whether that means taking classes, learning a new hobby, or improving your health and fitness.

- Travel and Adventure: Many retirees dream of traveling, whether it's exploring new countries or visiting places you've always wanted to see. Planning trips and adventures gives you something exciting to look forward to.

- Volunteering and Community Involvement: Giving back to your community can offer fulfillment and purpose. Whether it's mentoring, teaching, or working with local charities, volunteering is a meaningful way to spend your time.

Celebrate Your Milestones

As you work toward your retirement goals, it's important to celebrate milestones along the way. Whether it's completing a project, reaching a fitness goal, or visiting a dream destination, taking time to acknowledge these achievements can boost your motivation and happiness.

- Share with Family and Friends: Celebrating milestones with loved ones makes them even more special. You can host a gathering, share photos and stories, or reflect on your progress with those closest to you.

- Treat Yourself: When you reach a significant goal, don't hesitate to treat yourself! Whether it's a special dinner, a relaxing getaway, or buying something meaningful, reward yourself for the hard work and effort.

Practical Tip:

Create a "retirement bucket list" of things you've always wanted to do but didn't have time for during your working years. Whether it's travel, hobbies, or personal growth, write down your goals and plan ways to achieve them. Set smaller milestones along the way to track your progress and celebrate the successes.

Building a Legacy: Giving Back and Making a Difference

Retirement isn't just about enjoying your golden years—it's also a time to reflect on the legacy you want to leave behind. Many retirees find great fulfillment in using their time, resources, and wisdom to make a positive impact on others. Building a legacy could mean supporting your family, contributing to your community, or helping causes that matter to you.

Why Leaving a Legacy Matters

Building a legacy isn't just about financial inheritance; it's about the values, impact, and memories you leave behind. A legacy can take many forms—from creating a lasting family tradition to supporting charitable causes or mentoring others.

- Supporting Family: You might want to pass down family stories, traditions, or heirlooms to your children and grandchildren. Financially, you can help secure their future through gifts, trusts, or contributions to education and health.

- Philanthropy: Donating to charities, endowing scholarships, or contributing to causes that align with your values allows you to give back to society. Many retirees take pride in knowing they are helping future generations through their generosity.

- Mentorship and Volunteering: Your life experience and knowledge can be invaluable to others. Whether through formal mentoring programs, teaching, or informal guidance to friends and family, sharing your wisdom can leave a lasting impact on the people around you.

Ways to Build a Legacy

- Estate Planning: An important part of leaving a financial legacy is creating a will or trust to ensure that your assets are distributed according to your wishes. Speak with an estate planner or lawyer to help you navigate this process.

- Charitable Contributions: Consider setting up a donor-advised fund or making regular contributions to a cause that's close to your heart. Some retirees even choose to start their charitable foundations to continue their philanthropic work.

- Family Traditions and Values: Building a legacy can also mean passing down non-material things—like family traditions, cultural values, or important lessons. Write down your family history, create a photo album, or host gatherings that allow you to share stories and memories with your loved ones.

Practical Tip:

Think about the legacy you want to leave behind—whether through financial contributions, family traditions, or community service. Start by identifying the values most important to you, and explore ways you can give back or leave a lasting impact. If you're unsure where to begin, consider meeting with a financial planner or legal advisor to help you outline your estate and legacy plans.

Wrapping Up

Retirement is not just the end of your working life; it's the beginning of a new and exciting phase. By regularly reviewing your retirement plan, setting new goals, and thinking about the legacy you want to leave, you can ensure that this stage of life is both secure and fulfilling. Whether you're celebrating personal milestones, contributing to causes you care about, or sharing your wisdom with others, these final steps can help you create a retirement filled with purpose, joy, and lasting impact.

Retirement is your time to embrace all that life has to offer—so make it count!

Conclusion

Embracing the Next Chapter of Life

Retirement marks the beginning of a new chapter, filled with opportunities for personal growth, reflection, and fulfillment. It's a time to step back and appreciate all that you've accomplished throughout your life while also looking forward to the possibilities that lie ahead. As you navigate this next phase, staying open to new experiences and cultivating a positive outlook on retirement will allow you to embrace this journey with enthusiasm and grace.

Reflecting on Your Accomplishments and Goals

As you transition into retirement, it's essential to take a moment to reflect on the milestones you've achieved. Whether it's your career, raising a family, or overcoming personal challenges, you've already accomplished so much. Retirement is the perfect time to celebrate these successes and consider how they've shaped who you are today.

A Time to Appreciate Your Journey

Looking back on your life allows you to acknowledge the hard work and dedication that got you to this point. You've built a life full of experiences, relationships, and achievements that deserve recognition. Reflecting on these moments provides a sense of closure and accomplishment as you step into retirement.

- Celebrate Your Career: No matter the field or role, your career has been a significant part of your life. Reflect on the challenges you overcame, the skills you honed, and the contributions you made to your industry or community.

- Acknowledge Personal Growth: Your personal journey is just as important as your professional one. Think about the lessons you've learned, the obstacles you've overcome, and the personal development you've experienced along the way.

- Celebrate Family and Relationships: Family and friends have likely played a central role in your life. Reflect on the connections you've nurtured, the love you've given and received, and the ways these relationships have enriched your life.

Revisiting Your Goals

While retirement is often seen as the time to slow down, it's also a chance to revisit old dreams and set new goals. Reflect on the goals you've already achieved and think about those you still wish to pursue.

- Look at Unfinished Goals: Are there things you always wanted to do but didn't have the time for? Whether it's a hobby, travel destination, or learning a new skill, now is your chance to make it happen.

- Set Fresh Goals for This Stage: Retirement doesn't mean the end of goal-setting. It's the perfect time to redefine what success looks like for you. Maybe it's focusing on health and wellness, dedicating time to volunteer work, or simply enjoying more time with loved ones.

Practical Tip:

Create a journal or scrapbook where you can reflect on your life's journey. Document your achievements, cherished memories, and lessons learned. This personal reflection will not only help you celebrate the past but also inspire you to embrace the future.

Staying Open to New Experiences and Opportunities

While reflection is important, so is staying open to the endless possibilities that retirement can bring. This phase of life offers the freedom to explore new interests, try different activities, and engage with the world in ways you might not have considered before. Openness to change and new opportunities can make your retirement an exciting and enriching time.

Embrace a Growth Mindset

Retirement doesn't mean that learning or personal growth stops. In fact, it's a wonderful time to continue expanding your horizons. Whether through travel, education, or hobbies, being curious and willing to try new things can bring a renewed sense of purpose and excitement.

- Learn Something New: From taking online courses to picking up a new hobby like photography or painting, learning keeps your mind sharp and opens doors to experiences you never thought possible.

- Step Out of Your Comfort Zone: Whether it's trying a new type of fitness class, joining a book club, or traveling to an unfamiliar place, stepping out of your comfort zone can lead to new friendships and unexpected joys.

- Stay Active in the Community: Engage with local organizations, volunteer, or join a group that aligns with your passions. Staying socially connected is essential for both mental and emotional well-being.

Say Yes to Spontaneity

One of the great joys of retirement is the ability to be spontaneous. Without the rigid structure of a 9-to-5 job, you can embrace unexpected opportunities as they come your way.

- Take That Last-Minute Trip: Always wanted to visit a new city or country? With more flexible time, you can jump at the chance to travel on short notice or explore your local surroundings in a new way.

- Reconnect with Old Friends: If an old friend reaches out, say yes to a coffee date or a weekend getaway. Retirement offers the chance to rekindle relationships and spend time with those who matter to you.

- Be Open to New Social Circles: Whether through a club, volunteering, or a new hobby, retirement provides an opportunity to meet people from all walks of life. You never know where new friendships or connections might lead.

Practical Tip:

Create a "Yes List" of things you've always wanted to do but never had the chance. Include spontaneous activities, like taking a cooking class or going on a road trip. Keep this list visible, and when an opportunity arises, say yes without hesitation.

Encouraging a Positive Outlook on Retirement

Retirement is more than just leaving the workforce; it's entering a new chapter that can be full of joy, excitement, and fulfillment. Cultivating a positive mindset is key to fully embracing this phase of life. A cheerful outlook not only enhances your own experience but also inspires those around you, including family and friends.

Focus on Gratitude

Practicing gratitude has been shown to improve mental and emotional well-being. By focusing on the positive aspects of your life, you can shift your mindset toward appreciation and joy.

- Appreciate the Little Things: Take time each day to reflect on what you're grateful for. Whether it's your health, the love of family, or simply the beauty of nature, acknowledging these moments helps cultivate a sense of contentment.

- Keep a Gratitude Journal: Write down three things each day that you're thankful for. This practice encourages you to focus on the good in your life and can be a helpful reminder during times of transition or uncertainty.

Reframe Challenges as Opportunities

Retirement, like any life transition, comes with its own set of challenges. Whether it's adjusting to a new routine or facing health issues, how you approach these obstacles can make all the difference.

- Adopt a Problem-Solving Mindset: Instead of viewing challenges as setbacks, see them as opportunities to grow or learn something new. Embrace flexibility and find creative solutions to any hurdles you encounter.

- Seek Support When Needed: Don't hesitate to reach out to family, friends, or professionals when faced with difficulties. Sometimes, simply talking things through can shift your perspective and help you find a path forward.

Celebrate the Freedom of Retirement

Retirement is a time of freedom—freedom from work schedules, deadlines, and obligations. It's your opportunity to design the life you've always wanted.

- Enjoy the Flexibility: No more Monday meetings or rush-hour commutes! Now, you can create a routine that works for you. Whether it's leisurely mornings, afternoons spent with loved ones, or pursuing hobbies, enjoy the gift of time.

- Revel in Personal Choice: Retirement gives you the chance to prioritize what truly matters to you. Spend time doing what you love, whether that's traveling, gardening, or simply relaxing with a good book.

Practical Tip:

Start a daily or weekly ritual of reflecting on the positive aspects of your retirement. Whether through journaling, meditation, or a simple walk in nature, these moments of gratitude will help you maintain a positive outlook on this exciting chapter of life.

Wrapping Up: The Next Chapter Awaits

Retirement is not an end; it's the beginning of an exciting, rewarding, and fulfilling chapter of life. Reflect on all you've achieved, stay open to new experiences, and maintain a positive outlook. By doing so, you can make the most of your retirement, filled with growth, joy, and meaningful connections.

Embrace each day as an opportunity to explore new interests, set fresh goals, and leave a lasting legacy. Your retirement is your time—make it everything you've always dreamed of and more.

Appendices

The appendices serve as a valuable resource for those seeking practical tools and recommendations to enhance their retirement planning journey. They provide step-by-step guides, curated resources, and useful suggestions to help you navigate retirement with confidence. Whether you're just beginning to plan or already enjoying your retirement years, these appendices offer essential insights to help keep you on track.

Appendix A: Retirement Planning Checklist

Planning for retirement can feel overwhelming, but breaking it down into manageable steps ensures you cover all the important aspects. This checklist serves as a comprehensive guide to help you stay organized and confident as you approach this major life transition.

Step 1: Assess Your Financial Situation

- Calculate Your Net Worth: List your assets (savings, property, investments) and subtract your liabilities (debts, loans) to get a clear picture of your current financial standing.

- Review Income Sources: Identify all retirement income sources, such as Social Security, pensions, annuities, and any part-time work. Make projections to see how long these sources will sustain you based on your spending.

- Track Your Expenses: List your essential monthly expenses, including housing, healthcare, utilities, food, transportation, and leisure activities. This understanding will help you determine how much you'll need to sustain your lifestyle.

Step 2: Set Retirement Goals

- Define Your Retirement Lifestyle: Do you plan to travel, downsize, or pursue hobbies? Knowing how you want to spend your time helps estimate the cost of achieving your desired lifestyle.

- Create a Retirement Budget: Using the information from your expense tracking, develop a budget that accounts for your retirement goals. Be sure to include discretionary spending such as travel and entertainment.

Step 3: Maximize Retirement Savings

- Max Out Retirement Contributions: If you're still working, make sure to contribute the maximum to retirement accounts like a 401(k), IRA, or Roth IRA. Take advantage of any employer matching programs.

- Consolidate Retirement Accounts: Consider rolling over old 401(k) or IRA accounts into one to simplify management and reduce fees.

- Review Investment Strategy: Ensure your investments align with your risk tolerance and retirement timeline. As you near retirement, you may want to shift to more conservative investments.

Step 4: Plan for Healthcare Costs

- Review Health Insurance Options: Determine your eligibility for Medicare and consider whether you'll need supplemental insurance to cover additional medical costs.

- Estimate Long-Term Care Costs: Research the potential costs of long-term care and explore insurance options to help cover these expenses if needed.

Step 5: Create a Retirement Income Strategy

- Plan Your Withdrawal Strategy: Decide how and when to start withdrawing from retirement accounts. Develop a strategy to minimize taxes while ensuring a steady income stream.

- Consider Social Security Timing: Evaluate the best time to claim Social Security benefits based on your health, financial needs, and other income sources.

Step 6: Estate Planning

- Update or Create a Will: Ensure your will reflects your current wishes regarding asset distribution and guardianship if applicable.

- Establish Power of Attorney: Appoint someone you trust to make financial and healthcare decisions if you become unable to do so.

- Review Beneficiary Designations: Make sure your retirement accounts, insurance policies, and other assets have updated beneficiary information.

Appendix B: Resources for Financial Planning and Retirement

This section provides a curated list of resources to help guide you through the financial complexities of retirement planning. Whether you need expert advice, helpful calculators, or professional services, these resources can support your journey to financial security.

Financial Advisors and Retirement Planning Services

- Certified Financial Planners (CFPs): CFPs can help create a personalized retirement plan, review your investments, and develop strategies to maximize your savings. Look for professionals with retirement planning expertise.

- Fiduciary Advisors: Fiduciary advisors are legally obligated to act in your best financial interest. Seeking advice from a fiduciary ensures you receive unbiased guidance tailored to your needs.

Government Resources

- Social Security Administration (SSA): The SSA's website (ssa.gov) offers tools to estimate your benefits, check your earnings record, and learn about benefit timing.

- Medicare.gov: Provides detailed information on Medicare enrollment, benefits, and supplemental insurance options. It's essential for planning healthcare coverage in retirement.

Online Calculators and Tools

- Retirement Calculators: Websites like Vanguard, Fidelity, and T. Rowe Price offer retirement calculators to help estimate how long your savings will last and whether you're on track with your financial goals.

- Social Security Benefit Estimators: Use tools on the SSA website to better understand your future Social Security income based on retirement age and earnings history.

- Healthcare Cost Estimators: Resources like AARP's healthcare cost estimator help you project potential out-of-pocket medical expenses in retirement.

Appendix C: Recommended Online Tools

Continued learning is key to staying financially savvy and enjoying a fulfilling retirement. This appendix includes online courses and tools to deepen your understanding of retirement planning, personal finance, and how to make the most of your golden years.

Online Learning Platforms

- Coursera: Offers courses on personal finance, investing, and retirement planning from top universities like Stanford and Yale. Many courses are free, with an option to pay for certificates.

- Udemy: Provides affordable courses on topics from retirement planning and investing to hobbies and personal development.

- MasterClass: Features courses taught by world-renowned experts in fields ranging from writing and cooking to business and leadership, perfect for retirees looking to expand their knowledge.

Mobile Apps and Digital Tools

- Mint: A personal finance app that helps track spending, create budgets, and manage retirement accounts from one place.

- Personal Capital: Offers investment tracking tools, retirement calculators, and financial planning advice to help you stay on top of your financial future.

- YNAB (You Need A Budget): A budgeting app that helps control expenses, save more, and achieve financial goals during retirement.

Podcasts and Blogs

- "ChooseFI": A popular podcast offering tips on saving, investing, and achieving financial independence, with actionable insights for retirees.

- "The Retirement and IRA Show": A podcast focusing on retirement topics such as investments, tax efficiency, and income strategies.

- "AARP's Thinking About Retirement Blog": Provides up-to-date advice on retirement planning, Medicare, Social Security, and staying active in retirement.

Wrapping Up

These appendices serve as a go-to reference for practical tools, resources, and further reading as you embark on or continue your retirement journey. From checklists that keep your planning on track to resources for continued learning, these sections offer everything you need to secure a comfortable and fulfilling retirement. Keep this guide handy, revisit it as your retirement plans evolve, and take advantage of the wealth of information available to help you achieve your goals.

If this book has been valuable, please take out the time to drop a positive review about it. Reviews are very helpful for independent authors like me. THANK YOU!